D1634151

Down Your Street

by
Jean Gumbrell

Part Three

SAFFRON WALDEN

ISBN 0 9514542 2 6

Published by Jean Gumbrell,
Little Mortimers,
Ashdon,
Saffron Walden,
Essex. CN10 2NA

Printed by Hart-Talbot Printers,
Saffron Walden, Essex

Foreword

Looking again at the first two volumes compiled from Jean Gumbrell's Series 'Down Your Street' in the Saffron Walden Weekly News, I was struck by the amount of change which has taken place in the town during the short period of time since they were written in the mid to late 1980s.

In these days of constant change it is reassuring to be able to trace a thread of continuity within the community. Jean's well researched investigations around the streets of Saffron Walden allow us to do just that. Using an interesting mixture of personal reminiscence, historical fact and contemporary comment she builds up a picture of each street over a long period, while simultaneously showing us an instant picture of it at one point in time. Now with this third collection based on the original newspaper articles Jean brings us into the heart of the town covering some of the oldest streets and buildings.

This record of Saffron Walden, combining as it does memories of life here from early this century together with details of local families and their involvement in the life of the town, provides not only an interesting read but a valuable social history.

In his foreword to volume 2 John Shaw-Ridler noted the research value of Jean's first book to students of local history. This has proved to be just as true of the second volume and this third compilation will doubtless be equally appreciated now and increasingly so in the future.

Janet Crofts
SITE LIBRARIAN & ARTS DIRECTOR, SAFFRON WALDEN, 1996

*The contents of this book
and most of the
accompanying photographs
were first published
in the
Saffron Walden Weekly News*

from

*December 3rd 1987
to
March 7th 1991*

Preface

This is the third and final volume of my trilogy on Saffron Walden based on my series in The Saffron Walden Weekly News between December 1987 and March 1991. I hope that those who read my books will find some pleasure in them, perhaps a little instruction and bear with me for the mistakes I have made. It has, in the main, been a labour of love, tinged at times with sadness.

Jean Gumbrell

This book is dedicated to the people of Saffron Walden – past and present – because – Saffron Walden is a lovely place – and because – I believe people make places!

Acknowledgements

The author is indebted to the following people, without whose help this book would not have been possible.

The late Gordon Richards, former Editor of the Saffron Walden Weekly News, who suggested the series and was a tower of strength in those early days. Colin Moule, editor of the Saffron Walden Weekly News, for his help and moral support always. Di Pohlmann, sub-editor of the Saffron Walden Weekly News, for her continued help and invaluable support. Pam Jenner and all the staff of the Weekly News office at Saffron Walden for their unstinting co-operation. Cedric Tarrant, Picture Editor of Cambridge Newspapers for his co-operation and his photographers who have added so much to make the series more interesting.

The late Mary Whiteman, writer and journalist. The late Mr. Ken Lovatt, for the loan of old rating lists. The late Mr. Cliff Stacey local historian. Mr. John Shaw-Ridler, former Area Librarian for Essex County Council, Mrs. Jill Palmer former Area Librarian and Mrs. Janet Crofts, Site Librarian and Arts Director, and all her staff at Saffron Walden Library especially Information Librarian and Deputy Arts Director, Martyn Everett. Mr. Len Pole, Curator of Saffron Walden Museum. Sheila Jordain, retired Assistant Curator and Maureen Evans Press Officer of Saffron Walden Museum. Mr. Malcolm White, Town Clerk and his assistant Mrs. Helena Whysall. Local architect Mr. Donald Purkiss and local estate agent Mr. Bruce Munro. And to all who have given up precious time for interviews and taken endless trouble providing information.

The author also wishes to thank The Saffron Walden Weekly News. Essex County Council - Trustees of the Town Library Saffron Walden and David Campbell for permission to reproduce many of the photographs appearing in this book. Also all those who have loaned personal photographs.

She is grateful to Mr. Ken Wood Managing Director of Hart-Talbot Printers Ltd. and those members of his staff whose personal involvement in the production of this book and invaluable advice on all matters has been greatly appreciated.

She would like to thank all advertisers for their support.

And lastly her especial thanks to her husband, Michael, for all his support, encouragement and practical help.

Jean Gumbrell, Ashdon 1996

Sources

Department of Environment Notes on Listed Buildings (Town Library)

Harts' Almanacs 1853/1967 (Town Library)

Journals of the Saffron Walden Antiquarian Society

Mrs. Dorothy Monteith's Thesis (Town Library)

Saffron Crocus – Stanley Wilson (out of print)

Saffron Walden in Old Photographs – H. C. Stacey

Saffron Walden Personalities (Saffron Walden Museum Leaflet No. 12)

Saffron Walden Portrait of a Market Town – Anna Brooker & Mary Whiteman

Saffron Walden Then and Now – C. B. Rowntree (out of print)

Saffron Walden Rating Lists

David Self's Thesis on Saffron Walden (Town Library)

The Saffron Crocus (Saffron Walden Museum Leaflet No. 13)

Town Trail (Saffron Walden Museum Leaflet No. 1)

Various Pamphlets from Saffron Walden Town Library archives

x

Contents

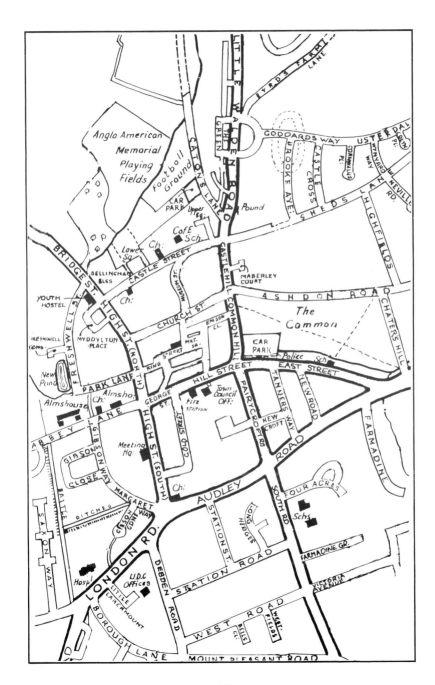

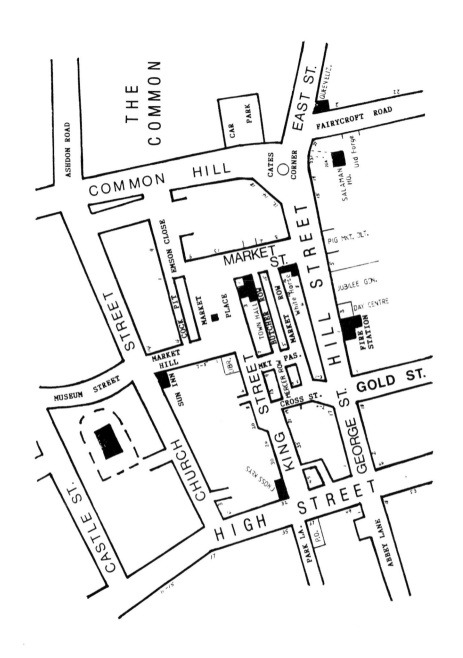

Saffron Walden Town Centre

Pictures
Down Your Street

CHAPTER ONE

Market Place

First published in the Saffron Walden Weekly News
December 3, 1987 - March 31, 1988

Undoubtedly the heart of Saffron Walden is to be found in its Market Place. But what we know as the Market Place today bears no resemblance to the Market Place of say - 200 years ago.

The actual history of Walden's market can be traced back to 1141, when Geoffrey de Mandeville moved the market from Newport to Walden in that year. Historian, Mrs. Dorothy Monteith writes, "the first stalls were set up outside the south castle walls on the slope leading down towards the Cam. Gradually houses were built to enclose a large rectangular market place..."

She continues. "No Cattle Market is recorded by name but cattle were sold in the open square. Complaints of cattle obstructing the entry of people living around the Market Place were recorded in the Court Rolls. The animals continued to be sold in this manner until a new cattle market was constructed in the 19th century."

Despite the new cattle market, horses were still sold in the Market Place at Horse Fairs, held twice yearly, until the first half of the 20th century. The dealers used the narrow streets such as King Street, George Street and Cross Street to "run" their horses.

In 1761, the Guild Hall, the Dolphin Inn and a dwelling house were all demolished to make way for a new Town Hall.

In 1818, the Market Cross which, for many years had had to be supported by scaffolding poles, was eventually pulled down, and the stocks removed to the junction of Castle Street and Museum Street. Later a lamp post was placed in the centre but this too, was removed to make way for the marble fountain which remains a feature of the Market Place today.

The Woolstaplers Hall was demolished in 1848 to be replaced by the Corn Exchange. And the latter decades of the 19th century saw yet another Town Hall built behind the spare elegance of the first, and the building we know as Barclays Bank, built on the site of the Angel Inn.

By the time the 20th century had dawned, the Market Place looked very much as it does today - that is as far as buildings are concerned. As the century progressed motor vehicles took the place of horse-drawn traffic, and eventually the Market Place became a car park on non-market days.

Market Place 1896.

Also, by this time, Market Day had been changed from Saturday to Tuesday. This was effected in 1892 after complaints from traders of the competition from the Cambridge Market which was also held on a Saturday.

2

But if the Market Place was the commercial heart of the town, it was also a great social amenity and a witness to numerous historical events both National and Civic. War and Peace. Royal Weddings and Political victories have all been celebrated or noted in some particular way by a gathering of townsfolk in the Market Place.

It is true that some of the events have been less commendable than others. It is believed that John Newman, a Pewterer from Kent and follower of John Bradford the Marian Martyr was burned at the stake in Walden Market Place. And here too, criminals and lesser offenders took their punishment in the stocks (big enough to hold ten men) and at the whipping post. Also Bull-baiting - one of the cruellest sports - continued here until well into the 18th century.

The marble fountain which has stood in the centre of the Market Place for well over a hundred years was presented to the town in 1863 by George Stacey Gibson and his mother Mrs. Wyatt George Gibson, to commemorate the marriage of Prince of Wales (later Edward VII) to Princess Alexandra of Denmark.

Designed by the architect John Francis Bentley, when a pupil of Henry Clutton the distinguished architect (so it is said), it is believed to have been exhibited at the London Exhibition held in 1862.

A close inspection of the fountain reveals four carved panels depicting biblical scenes. By the 1970s these panels and the fountain itself were showing signs of wear, so in 1974 the Town Council asked for tenders to carry out the renovation. Messrs. Rattee and Kett of Cambridge were finally chosen to do the work at a rough estimate of £7,000.

———— • ————

Now let us look at the buildings surrounding the Market Place starting with the modern architecture of Boots the Chemists. Throughout the centuries the Rose & Crown stood on this site watching the changing fortunes of Saffron Walden. Just how many centuries we are not certain. (C.B. Rowntree - The Essex Countryside Magazine 1953 - suggests the inn dated from 1359 - possibly earlier.)

3

He dates the inn by the bunch of grapes, still to be seen suspended on the façade of Boots. The bunch, measuring three feet in height, is carved from one solid block of oak, and was, says Mr. Rowntree, the earliest common sign of all inns. During a gale in the 1940s the sign crashed to the ground, and after that was, for many years, stored in a stable at the rear of the inn. Finally it was rescued in 1950 to be put on display at an exhibition of relics and records at the Town Hall.

According to C.B. Rowntree early records refer to the inn as "The Rose." Entries in old rating lists also use this same name on occasions. The evidence for the name-change from The Rose to the Rose & Crown is, according to Mr. Rowntree, suggested by the fact that Henry Duke of Lancaster organised a revolt against Richard II, forcing him to abdicate, and taking his place on the throne as Henry IV. The emblem of the Duchy of Lancaster being a red rose, the Crown being added to the inn's name when Henry ascended the throne - the manor of Saffron Walden being part of the Duchy of Lancaster.

Whatever the origins of its name, just as the Market Place itself was the place where the townsfolk gathered to mourn or celebrate, so was the Rose & Crown the chosen venue for other, perhaps more parochial, happenings.

It was at The Rose that the Woolstaplers feasted after their noisy procession through the town and neighbouring villages, accompanied by Mayor and Corporation, plus band, followed by shepherds and shepherdesses. A custom which continued until late in the 18th century.

It was at The Rose in the 18th century, that Thomas Pennystone, steward of Audley End, collected tithes from the tenants whilst enjoying his beef and ale dinner.

Here, generations of farmers met on Market Days, to talk shop, strike bargains, gossip and enjoy a midday meal. In 1860 the Rose & Crown served a half guinea meal at 1 o'clock on Market Days (Saturdays) which, it was said, was well-patronised. (This was in the days when half a guinea - about 50p - represented a farm worker's wages for a week.)

The Conservative Club was first inaugurated at the Rose & Crown (sometime before 1885) and most of the important

4

auctions in the town took place here, as well as the meetings of many local organisations.

It was the town's premier hotel. Many of the older generation still remember the "omnibus" which collected third class railway passengers for Audley End Station. (The more elegant carriage and pair was for the use of first class passengers only). The horses belonging to the inn were also used to pull the fire engines at one time.

Up to the 20th century the Rose & Crown had always been privately owned. The last owners - the Gibsons - obtained it from the son of the draper and grocer, William Wiseman, after he had run into debt (see page 7). The Gibsons sold it to Trust Houses Ltd., about 1915, and it is as a Trust House that most people remember it.

Mr. Edward Griffith reliving his memories of staying at the Rose & Crown in 1929 when an undergraduate at Cambridge (Essex Countryside Magazine) writes of the key to the hotel's success.

"It had an informal relaxed atmosphere, not too high faultin' with courteous old-fashioned type of service. If the main lounge became a trifle crowded we could retreat to the seldom used residents' lounge, plentifully supplied with bound volumes of Punch from around 1900 and copies of the Farmer and Stockbreeder."

The last visit Mr. Griffith, now a married man, paid to the Rose & Crown was October 1969 when arrangements for the Christmas festivities were already posted up.

Christmas 1969 lives on in the memories of all who love Saffron Walden. When Boxing Day dawned the old Rose & Crown had been reduced to a burned-out shell. Eleven people had perished in the fire.

The cause of the fire has never been properly established, but the general opinion was, that a faulty electric plug belonging to a television set, caught fire.

Conservationists fought long and hard to preserve all that was left of this much loved hotel - the façade. Authority said it was too dangerous to preserve. But the Conservationists said they could prove Authority wrong. Authority won. Saffron Walden lost its best-loved landmark and with it went a whole way of life.

5

The site was bought by Boots the Chemists who payed lip-service to the memory of the old coaching inn by incorporating the shell canopy that had once graced the front entrance in a wall at the rear of the store at the same time suspending the gilded bunch of grapes from the façade.

Nevertheless the Rose & Crown remains an ever-present ghost in the Market Place of Saffron Walden. It is little wonder that those who enjoyed the intimacy of an old-fashioned market town, and now mourn the passing of the old days, frequently say - it all started with the fire at the Rose & Crown!

——— • ———

The splendid Victorian-Tudor façade of Barclays Bank in Saffron Walden adds a certain dignity and unity to the architectural hotch-potch of the Market Place.

The Bank was built in 1874 on the site of the old Angel Inn. The Angel - previously called "The Horn" - adjoined the Rose & Crown, and dated back to at least the 16th century.

Wiseman's shop, demolished in 1874 to make way for Barclays Bank.

In the 18th century both buildings were owned by William Flower who decided to incorporate the upper storey of the Angel into the Rose & Crown and convert the ground floor into two shops. The shops were bought by William Wiseman, draper and grocer, who converted them into one and, in 1796, also bought the Rose & Crown.

When William Wiseman died both properties were inherited by his son who, unfortunately speculated heavily in malt at the wrong time. He was declared bankrupt and both properties came into the possession of his bankers - the Gibsons.

The Gibson Bank had been founded in 1824 in opposition to Searles' Bank - the only bank in the town at that time. (The Searles, seeing how prosperous the malting industry had made the Gibsons, had set themselves up as maltsters. This infuriated the Gibsons and they retaliated by founding their own Bank. Within a year of the Gibson Bank starting up Searles' Bank ran into financial difficulties and was forced to close down, leaving the field wide-open to their rivals.)

The founding partners of "Gibson and Company, Saffron Walden and North Essex Bank" were - Atkinson Francis Gibson, Wyatt George Gibson, Thomas A. Catlin and Nathaniel Catlin. Their first premises were probably at No.53 High Street, but later they moved to Market Hill.

The Gibson Bank flourished. Their Bank Notes were freely circulated and by 1838 they had sold all their brewery interests and confined their business activities to running the Bank.

In 1874, after 50 years in Market Hill, they took possession of the Angel and the Rose & Crown from Wiseman. The result was that the historic Angel was demolished and in its place they built the present-day monument to Mammon.

The wellknown Victorian architect William Eden Nesfield was commissioned to carry out the work. Better known for his country houses, the Bank remains his only commercial commission.

The Bank remained in the Gibson family until 1862 when, after the death of both Francis Edward Gibson and Wyatt George Gibson in that year, George Stacey Gibson - Wyatt

7

George's son - found himself the sole surviving partner. Thus, in May 1863 he took his brother-in-law, William Murray Tuke and his cousin, Edmund Birch Gibson, into partnership.

William Murray Tuke, son of Samuel Tuke, tea merchant of York, was grandson of James Hack, one of the founders of the banking firm of Hack, Dendy & Co., of Chichester. (His brother, James Hack Tuke, was a partner in the Hertfordshire Hitchin Bank.)

Interior of Barclays Bank at the turn of the century.

After George Stacey Gibson's death in 1883, the Bank was amalgamated with Barclay & Co. Ltd., in 1896. William Murray Tuke and Edmund Birch Gibson were both appointed local Directors with Edmund Birch Gibson chosen to represent the old Bank on the Board of the new one.

By this time William Favill Tuke - the eldest son of William Murray - had also joined the firm and he too, became a Local Director of Barclay & Co. Ltd., at the time of the amalgamation. Later, in 1904, he also became an Inspector, later still, Chairman from 1934 to 1936. His son,

Anthony William Tuke and grandson, Sir Anthony Favill Tuke, were, in time, both to become Chairmen of Barclays and to this day Sir Anthony is still on the Board of Directors.

Saffron Walden was one of the Local Head Offices of Barclay & Co. Ltd., from 1896 until 1912, when its branches were merged into the Cambridge District. Edmund Birch Gibson's son, Alexander, remained as Local Director for Saffron Walden only, until his retirement in 1919.

Although Banks and banking have changed considerably since the Gibsons built their Bank in the Market Place in 1874, some things have, surprisingly remained the same.

Externally the building has changed little. Internally the open counter tops are gone, and the clerks no longer sit on high stools at sloping desks illuminated by gas or oil lamps. But the original fine carved panelling and the fireplace with its splendid tiles may still be seen in the main entrance of the Bank. And if you visit Barclays around Christmas time you will be greeted by the welcome blaze of a real open fire. A Dickensian touch of nostalgia perhaps, but none the worse for that.

It has always been essentially "the farmers' bank" and many of its former Managers are still remembered with esteem and affection in agricultural circles.

One of these is Mr. Dennis Aves who first came to the Saffron Walden Branch of Barclays as a young 25 year-old ledger clerk in 1950.

Mr. Aves has vivid memories of his early days in Saffron Walden, he says, 'in those days we all worked with pen and ink and all the casting was done in our heads. And all the interest on every draft or deposit account had to be worked out by hand from a book.

Yes - we had to be pretty good at figures! Although I do remember we did actually have one adding machine which was manually operated.

Balance nights were the worst! On those nights we had to work extremely hard - usually until about two o'clock in the morning. This happened twice a year - on the 30th June and 31st December. And the 31st December was by far the worst of all! We always welcomed the New Year in at the Bank.

9

After we had finished the day's work, we had to sit down and "prove" the ledgers, then rule off everyone's statement and bring down a new balance for the next half year. But those were the days of the Rose & Crown - so we would pop next door every now and again for a bit of a rest and a little refreshment!

At that time the Manager was Mr. Louis Jeeves. He was a very musical man, and extremely well-known in the town. He was Church organist; Musical Director of the Saffron Walden Operatic Society, and also conductor of the Male Voice Choir. He was Manager for quite a long time, from about 1947 to 1960 if I remember rightly. And on Balance Nights he would always treat us to a special tea with sandwiches and cakes.

Working in the Bank has always been a team effort, and there was always a lot of fun with plenty of teasing.

When I first came to Saffron Walden we only had two ladies on the staff - and it was a different life. Now it has swung round completely.

There was one cashier, I remember, called Bunny Hunt. He had been a cashier for years - but that was the general rule in those days. Bunny served quite a lot of the farmers, especially on Fridays when the farmers came in to collect the wages for their workers. Farm workers' wages were a lot lower then than they are now, and the farmers needed a lot of silver coins to make up the wages. So instead of handing out the silver to the farmers, Bunny would leave a large pile of silver on the counter top, and the farmers would just help themselves! Of course, those were the days of open counter tops - long before we had grills.

All the old bank notes had to be returned to the Bank of England. This meant that two of us would walk down the street to the General Post Office with something like ten to fifteen thousand pounds each tucked under our arm - and we would never think anything of it!

The thing which has always stuck in my mind is, people were so honest and trustworthy in those days. They would always come back and tell us if there were any errors made out in their favour. But I would say that this honesty still exists today - there is just a small element, unfortunately, who are not quite so trustworthy. Most people however are as honest as the day is long!'

Dennis Aves stayed at the Saffron Walden Branch of Barclays for twelve years, working his way up from ledger clerk to cashier and then on to Securities Clerk, all the time studying for his Banking Exams to eventually become an Associate of the Institute of Bankers.

He left Walden to become Chief Clerk at the Royston Branch, later Manager of Great Shelford, and then Manager of the Cherry Hinton Road Branch at Cambridge. Finally, he returned to Saffron Walden as Manager in 1975.

After a total of 23 years in Saffron Walden Branch, Mr. Aves retired in July 1986. He now lives in a village close by and still enjoys taking an active part in the life of the town. This includes Rotary, acting as treasurer to several local charities, playing a lot of golf and being a director of the Saffron Walden Herts & Essex Building Society.

——— • ———

It is difficult to envisage a farm situated in the north-eastern corner of the Market Place of present-day Walden. Yet rating lists in 1757 indicate that there was a farm on this spot.

According to Department of Environment records, No.6 Market Place - The Midland Bank - was built in the 19th century, and the adjoining building - now an antique shop - dates back from the 16th and 17th centuries. Walk around the corner of this building and you will see that the whole structure does indeed, resemble an old farmhouse with a massive chimney.

Could this possibly be the house of the statesman and scholar, Sir Thomas Smyth, who was born in Walden in 1514, and lived in a house on the north-east corner of the Market Square? As this particular building dates back to the early 16th century, this seems quite feasible. (Later, Sir Thomas Smyth moved to the Priory - a house facing the Common). (See Chapter Three - Common Hill).

Thomas Smyth's scholastic career began at the Grammar School in Castle Street and continued at Cambridge where he was financed as one of Henry VIII's scholars.

11

After graduating he became Professor of Civil Law at Cambridge, a distinguished mathematician, philosopher and astronomer. He also wrote a tract on the correct pronunciation of the English language and devised a more comprehensive alphabet of 29 letters (made up of 19 Roman, 4 Greek and 6 Saxon).

During the reign of Edward VI he was extremely active in the reformed church, and in 1549 became Secretary of State. Unfortunately later that year he fell from favour, lost his office and was confined to the Tower of London for a short time.

Returning to favour once more he was made Ambassador to France for both Edward VI and Elizabeth I. And it was during Elizabeth's reign that he again became Secretary of State.

The first farmer recorded in the rating lists on this site is a Mr. Mapletoft. However, by 1790, Mapletoft vacated the farm for some reason and the name Joseph Martin appears in the rating lists.

The entry for Joseph Martin reads:- "land - stables in the Market Place!" Later entries for Joseph Martin give "messuage, farm, land and lime kiln!" So somewhere on this site - probably near Emson Close - there was a lime kiln.

Joseph Eedes succeeds Joseph Martin in 1802, but now there is no mention of a farm. Later however, when Joseph Eedes is deceased his widow continues on in the house, and we find the entry:- "Mrs. Eedes - house, stables, chaisehouse and gardens." This good lady continued to live at the house until 1827, when the entry for that year states "house unoccupied." Also, about this time the house next door - No.6 Market Place - was built for John Player by William Robinson, a wellknown local surveyor and builder.

John Player was one of the town's great benefactors, born in 1796 of a Walden family living in Deptford. His distinguished career in the Civil Service started by his entry as a humble clerk. But ill-health forced him to retire early to the more favourable clime of Saffron Walden, where he lived first at No.73 High Street, and then No.6 Market Place.

Gradually he absorbed himself into the public life of the town, and in 1829 was appointed Overseer of the Poor. His allotment scheme for the appropriation of land for use by the poor was one of the first in the country and aroused a great deal of interest. He also promoted many local charities; was an active member of the Horticultural Society and, together with Jabez Gibson, became a major force behind the founding of the Museum.

A lifelong member of the Abbey Lane Meeting House, as soon as nonconformists were allowed to hold public office in 1836, he was elected Mayor.

He was also a man of letters. As well as writing several small volumes of poetry, his series of essays - Saffron Walden and its Vicinity - must be the earliest version of Down Your Street ever to be written!

He died in 1846, and for a few years his widow lived on at No.6. After that for the next forty years the house appears to have had a number of owners and tenants - including Joshua Clarke the maltster who rented the property to Herbert Taylor.

No. 6 Market Place,
Dr. Frederick Goadby's house
– now the Midland Bank.

In 1888 we find Walter Emson living at No.6. He was a member of the Emson family, who were notable farmers in the area, and one of whom, John Emson, built the elegant house on the site of the Town Malt Mill. No.6 remained in the hands of the Emson family until about 1915. From then it changed hands once or twice until the eminent theologian and scholar Dr. Frederick Goadby bought it. (Several of his works are to be found in the Town Library).

Dr. Goadby lived here until the 1950s, then in 1965 The Saffron Walden Benefit Building Society moved from Lime Tree Passage to No.6 and for the next nine years occupied the premises. (Down Your Street - Part Two - pages 195-6.)

When the Saffron Walden Building Society moved to their purpose built premises in Market Street in 1974, the Midland Bank took over No.6 and has remained there ever since.

The Manager, Mr. John Mayhew told me that, although the building was eminently suitable for a bank, certain alterations had to be made. This includes one of the most sophisticated and up-to-date security systems in the country.

Although he could not, of course, divulge the extremely advanced alarm system, he demonstrated one or two features - which included a bullet-proof screen hidden in the open-counter top, which protects the bank clerks in case of trouble.

---— • ——

An early painting of the Market Place in the 18th century, by Francis Gosse, illustrates the full beauty of the elegant house which was built close to the Town Malt Mill (now Eaden Lilley fashion store).

The Town Malt Mill, worked by horse power, dated from medieval times. It was at one time the manorial Malt Mill, where local brewers were obliged to have their malt made on penalty of a fine. Later the Mill was purchased by the Town Chamberlain and leased out to a miller. Hamond Carter is believed to have been the first miller to lease the Mill in 1574.

It has also been suggested that John Emson was the miller at one time although his name does not appear in the rating lists for the Market Place until 1809. Entries before that date give the name of Samuel Parke (or Parker) who had first, a house and shop on this site - 1790 - later in 1796 - house and land.

Samuel Parke(r) died in 1806 leaving his widow to occupy the house until 1807 when the name Samuel Poole appears with John Emson taking over from Samuel Poole in 1809.

Writer and Journalist Mary Whiteman, in her history of the Emson family believes that John Emson added the roofed verandah and other refinements to the already handsome building. This was probably about 1834 - the year he became Mayor. He appears to have rented the property from "Dudley Parke" presumably one of Samuel Parke's heirs until 1822 when he eventually buys it.

The entry for 1822 refers to a shop, as well as warehouse and stables. (There had been no mention of a shop since 1790 when the premises were in the possession of Samuel Parke.)

There is a note at the bottom of the rating lists for 1834, to the effect that John Emson sold some of his property to improve the rest. This strengthens the belief that this was when he added certain improvements to the house, including the carved wooden likeness of himself under the decorated canopy of the side entrance fronting Market Hill.

In the entry for the next year, John Emson owns not only his house and shop(s) - "as improved" - but also sundry land as well as a barn and land - all in the Market Place, including a brick kiln! By 1837 the rating list entries read - "John Emson & Son" - and by 1840 it is "John Emson & Sons" and a coach house and loft have been added to the property. Obviously the fortunes of the Emson family were on the way up!

John Emson's three sons, Charles, Edmund and Frank were all scholars who helped to record some of the history of Saffron Walden. Charles translated from the Latin, The Cartulary of Walden Abbey, Edmund translated early Walden Deeds and Frank wrote a history of the town and its neighbourhood. He also wrote "Ye Comick Guide and Historie of Saffron Walden" and "Our Town, or the Life at Slowborough". (All to be found in the Town Library).

The next significant entry in the rating lists relating to this building is in 1841 when "John Emson and Sons" is changed to "John Green Emson and Frederick Emson" under the heading of Occupier, and "John Emson" under Owner. Later

15

the 1851 Census list gives only the name of Frederick Emson "Draper and Grocer" - no mention of John Green Emson.

By 1856 Jane Emson (John Emson senior's widow?) owns the property, whilst John Green Emson occupies the house, and warehouse etc. The Malt Mill however, now described

Stebbing Leverett's at the turn of the century – now Eaden Lilley.

as "empty" is in the joint ownership of both the Emson and the Gibson family.

Joshua Clark occupied the Malting in 1859 - although Jane Emson is recorded as being the owner. There is now no mention of Frederick.

For the next 20 years or so - until her death sometime between 1875-6 - Jane Emson owns the property but the house and adjoining shop are let out to Joseph Scott, later in 1879 Stebbing Leverett, (See Chapter Five - Market Hill).

John Green Emson inherits the property, but continues to let both house and shop to Stebbing Leverett, and the name Frank Evenett Emson now appears alongside that of John Green - presumably the latter's son. And, according to rating lists, Stebbing Leverett carries on the drapery side of his business on this site well into the 20th century.

It would appear that John Green Emson died about 1900-01, the property passing to John Evenett Emson who, later sold both business and property to Ernest William Tanner. Ernest William Tanner was the son of J.W. Tanner founder of several grocery and drapery shops in various parts of North Essex - Thaxted (run by William S. Tanner) - Bardfield (Fred Tanner) and Great Dunmow (Hugh Tanner).

According to Ernest William's son, Mr. E.B.T. Tanner, who lived in Saffron Walden from 1905 until 1928 or thereabouts the name "Emson" was retained in order to have the advantage of the goodwill of that name, since Emsons had been trading in the area for about two hundred years.

Early advertisements for Emson Tanner show the old buildings of the Malt Mill, and how Gayhomes gradually evolved from what at first appears to be a dilapidated outbuilding to a warehouse, and later what it is today. Of course in those days the public weighbridge would have still been standing in front of the building. It had been placed there in 1812 and removed in 1928.

Alderman Ernest William Tanner was a great local character. The late Stanley Wilson in his book, "Saffron Crocus", describes him as having "no fear and little tact."

"Physically," he writes, "he was a fine, fat and fit man, full of the joy of living, with a Peter Pan sense of subconscious mischief. At weddings, public ceremonies and funerals he was a real fine fellow with his silk top hat and frock coat with tails, a man bound to be noticed even in a large crowd".

It was E.W. Tanner (he was always referred to as "E.W. Tanner") who blended a special brand of tea to suit the extremely hard water in the Saffron Walden area. And, according to Stanley Wilson, "knew the grocery trade through and through."

E.W. Tanner died at the age of 90 in 1962.

Mrs. Margaret Warner (née Smith) of Godmanchester, who was born in Debden Road, Saffron Walden has been kind enough to write down her memories of working at Emson Tanner's for me.

17

She writes:- "I started work at Emson Tanner's as the office girl in 1937. In those days I was a very shy young lady, just out of school.

My immediate boss was a Miss Mansfield who came from Cambridge. She was Mr. Tanner's private secretary, and had taught me shorthand and typing, and had also been responsible for getting me the job at Emson Tanner's.

I remember my first morning at work. I was petrified at finding so many young men around the place. One in particular was the 15 year-old office boy - Fred Warner. It was his job to answer the telephone, make the tea and fetch the buns (which incidentally were a 1d each) from Anthony's in the High Street. He was affectionately known as "Warner" to everyone, and although I was far too shy to speak to him at that stage, I was extremely concerned about his hair, which used to stand up on end as if he'd had a fright!

I remember remarking to a friend that if Warner did something about his hair he would be quite a nice looking boy.

One day, Bill Johnson, one of the senior clerks said, - Warner. I am not having your hair looking like that anymore! And he went out and bought a bottle of Brylcreem from the nearby hairdresser to smooth down young Warner's locks. From that time onwards Warner always looked very smart and well-groomed, and still does - because he has never stopped using Brylcreem from that moment.

I managed to overcome my shyness with Warner when, one day he came into my office and said - I'm afraid Miss Smith you are getting very rude in your old age! You have put an S instead of a W in the address on this letter! And when I tell you that the letter was addressed to Messrs. Newman and Whitmore I am sure you will understand why I blushed to the roots of my hair!

After that I ceased to be in awe of him and our friendship blossomed.

It was a very busy office, but everyone was very friendly and kind and I soon felt at home. The head of the Company was Mr. E.W. Tanner, a Justice of the Peace and a very respected figure in town. He would come into our office to dictate letters to Miss Mansfield, and I often wondered how she coped as she followed him all round the warehouse taking notes which would all have to be read back and I have no doubt - changed! Little did I know then that, one day, I too would have to take notes from the formidable Mr. Tanner!

After a little while, Edna Badman, a schoolfriend, daughter of Ben Badman, Manager of the Labour Exchange, came to work in the office alongside me. We had lots of fun together, and although the wages were extremely low, we nevertheless enjoyed the work.

With the coming of World War two the young men were gradually called up and replaced by girls. Another great friend of mine Beryl Braybrooke - still a great friend - joined us. I taught her to type and use the switchboard. And I remember well, once to my horror I heard her addressing Messrs. Rattee and Kett as "Rattee and Cat"! But although I promptly corrected her, we both just collapsed with laughter - and that seemed to be the pattern of most days - plenty of fun and laughter, despite the fact that we worked extremely hard.

On Friday nights we had to work late in order to get the "offers" out. The offers were the prices of the goods we had on offer the following week, which the travellers (they were not called reps in those days) took with them on their rounds, and which were notified to all our customers. For this we had to use an old duplicating machine and more often than not we managed to get ink all over ourselves as well as on our clothes.

But all this time my friendship with Warner was growing. We found we had a lot in common - music especially - we both played the piano. I used to invite him to my home to spend an evening with us, and mother used to make a great fuss of him and feed him up with coffee and cakes.

As the war progressed the work in the office became more difficult and complicated. Food rationing was now in force and we had to work in conjuction with the Food Office for quite a lot of the time and often had to work on Saturday mornings.

Of course all of us girls were exempt from war service

Staff at Emson Tanner's 1940s. Left to right, Mary Harding, Hazel Shelley, Valerie Jacobs, Audrey Brooks.

because we worked in a Food Store, and this pleased my parents because I was an only child.

In 1939 Warner and I became engaged and then it was his turn to be called-up for the forces. And I well remember the morning he walked past the office with his father on the way to catch the train. From then onwards for the next few years we only had letters to look forward to.

We had some very sad moments in the office when we learned that John Palmer and George Auger had been killed. John had been in the office and George had worked in the warehouse before they had joined the forces. And I remember the moment when Mr. Tanner came into my office to dictate a letter of sympathy to Mrs. Palmer - John's mother.

By this time Miss Mansfield had left and I often took dictation from Mr. Tanner. I used to be absolutely petrified that I would not be able to read my shorthand back and often cheated by writing in longhand.

Warner and I were married on December 18th 1941. He had 48 hours leave and when he returned to his regiment he was sent straight abroad. He was only 19 years old at the time - one of the youngest men to be sent overseas.

I continued to work on at Emson Tanner's until Warner returned in 1945. And it was a very sad day for me when I left the office. I had so many happy memories of the place and had made so many friends."

Emson Tanner continued to operate as a wholesale grocers until the 1950s.

In 1962 - the year of E.W. Tanner's death - after lying empty for sometime, the building was bought by Mr. Aubrey Rumsey and his wife, Mona, who decided to put their three Saffron Walden enterprises under one roof. Previously, they had had a furniture shop on the corner of King Street (now Patricia's), a bedding centre on the corner of Abbey Lane with a nursery shop next door (now Expression and Panache).

Rumseys 1981.

After six months renovating the old building, Rumseys opened in style with the television personality of the day - Mr. Michael Miles - performing the ceremony.

21

For the next 23 years Rumseys furnishing store became an important amenity in the Market Place. But in 1985 after 31 years in Saffron Walden, and 28 years previously in Leytonstone, Aubrey Rumsey closed the doors of his furnishing establishment for the very last time. And once again, one of the most elegant buildings in Saffron Walden, looked out across the bustle of the Market Place with a sad, empty-eyed stare.

Then in 1987, an old-established family firm of Cambridge drapers came to Saffron Walden - Eaden Lilley - and opened up their fashion store in the sadly neglected building. It was a fitting gesture for Saffron Walden because Eaden Lilley's origins can be traced back as far as 1695 in Cambridge.

Eaden Lilley brought elegance and glamour into the lives of many local ladies. They discovered the great joy of wandering through a shop filled with lovely clothes and accessories. There was also the added pleasure of sitting high amongst the rooftops of the town, in what was once, no doubt, the servants' quarters in John Emson's day, drinking coffee or tea and indulging in a little diet-wrecking.

———— • ————

We now come to the Corn Exchange, circa 1847, described as having been built in a "classical" manner and also "in a tasteless and jolly Italianate style" (Pevsner).

Certainly whatever merits the Corn Exchange possesses, it would have been better for Saffron Walden if the old Woolstaplers' Hall, which it replaced, had been left standing. This was a magnificent timber-framed building, believed to be similar to the one in Lavenham, Suffolk.

The Woolstaplers' Hall was demolished in 1844, and the architect Richard Tress was commissioned to design a new building, this time to deal with the fast-developing trade in Corn.

Richard Tress 1809-1875, was a distinguished London architect, responsible for the designing and altering of many notable buildings in the City of London. There is also evidence to support the theory that he was responsible for having designed the west front extensions to Hill House for

George Stacey Gibson at the time of the building of the Corn Exchange.

For a hundred years the Corn Exchange flourished in the capacity for which it was intended. And then gradually, changes in the organisation of the Corn Trade led to its decline. And what had once been a thriving centre of commerce became a venue for rummage sales; dances; roller skating; auction sales and the storage of market stalls.

But social events had always been part of the role it played in the life of the community. It was here that heroes returning from the wars were feasted. And it was at the Corn Exchange that Coronations and Jubilees were celebrated - even the opening of a new Co-operative store.

Local Estate Agent and Auctioneer, Mr. Bruce Munro in his "Profile of the Corn Exchange" gives an extremely graphic account of the latter years of the Corn Exchange before it became the Library and Arts Centre. He has very kindly granted me permission to quote extensively from this work:-

"Each Tuesday market day," he writes, "more than twenty stands with sloping desk tops bearing the name of a local

Woolstaplers' Hall demolished in 1844 to make way for the Corn Exchange.

23

corn merchant were placed in four rows. In the afternoon the merchants arrived, took up their stance, elbows on desk tops and awaited their farmer customers to bring samples of corn and seed to buy and sell.

It was a good place to meet - farmers, the auctioneer, the insurance agents and the N.F.U. secretary - all met, laughed, dealt and perhaps drank in the Rose & Crown opposite - open all the afternoon for the purpose of succouring those persons attending the public market.

The Market Place offices, on either side of the Grand Entrance, served - on the left as a Corn Merchants - and on the right as the Weekly News Offices." (This is where "Under the Clock" - which has recently made a welcome re-appearance in the Weekly News - originated.)

"The comings and goings of Mayors, Aldermen and Burgesses to encourage, cajole or kill the Editor - a wellknown local personage - was a common sight," continues Mr. Munro.

Mr. Ernest Jennings with assistant Roy Fisher conducting an auction in the Corn Exchange.

24

"Not least of the regular functions to be held in the Corn Exchange were the monthly Furniture Sales which were held by local auctioneers. These were auctions of household furniture and antiques. Good for business, convenient for setting up a home and good entertainment if the Corn Exchange was not too hot or too cold.

In high summer the building was so hot that we used to spray the glass roof with lime wash with the aid of a stirrup pump.

The only heating for winter was a Tortoise stove at the Market Place end, the heat from which was rapidly drawn into the Market Place as the hefty swing doors, that pushed or pulled, swung to and fro - often catapulting people in the opposite direction to that intended! One petite lady landed on the top of the fountain!

One hot July day there was a cloud burst, rain and hailstones penetrated, nearly drowning the Auctioneer.

Five hundred lots was not unusual - we used to lot up until 10 o'clock the night before. The sales were an institution - the same dealers usually attended together with the same onlookers. One pregnant lady who never missed, was there at one sale and back with her offspring at the next. Strangely enough, he didn't become an auctioneer.

The porters were great characters. The greatest was Bill Johnson. He was head porter in the Cattle Market, and hailed, I believe, from Shropshire and was always referring to doing things - 'this road.' A lover of good ale - the true and proper drink of English men and market porters - if he was occasionally missing from the Corn Exchange and if he was not in the Cattle Market, then as like as not he'd be in the White Horse or the Dog and Gun - chatting up potential buyers and sellers - you understand?

Bill Johnson was ably assisted by the brothers Cox - Neville and Ernie. Neville had a secondhand anything business in a yard and barns where Martins' shop is in Cross Street. (Down Your Street - Part Two - pages 160-162). He used to keep saying 'yes, yes, yes,' whilst Ernie's call sign was 'what do you mean?'

A few chords from 'Ancient & Modern' on the many pianos by the resident pianist, Mr. Adam Wright - a frequent purchaser who lived to be a 100 - revealed their quality and value!

Regular dealers included a grand Dickensian character - Bill Mares - from Sewards End. He was a large round gentleman with small gold spectacles. Anything which did not sell was knocked down to him for a shilling - he rarely objected, but on the occasions he did, then Neville Cox took it - if both objected it was fairly certain to be unsaleable and had to be taken to the dump.

Many owners of valuable eighteenth century pieces today have cause to be grateful to Corn Exchange Sales.

Thirty years ago you could not give away Victorian oil lamps, stuffed chairs and the like and now - today - well!"

——— • ———

By the late 1960s the Corn Exchange had become a white elephant, an expensive embarrassment the Borough Council were eager to dispose of. They were looking for a buyer who would demolish the building and put something bright and attractive in its place like a multi-storey car park or huge supermarket. Controversy raged!

What started out as a purely local issue eventually reached national proportions. If it had not been for a far-sighted band of people like Edward Bawden R.A., Olive Cook, the late Stanley Wilson and many others, the Corn Exchange would not be standing today!

The argument for saving the Corn Exchange received support from many distinguished architects - Sir Hugh Casson, Sir Frederick Gibberd, Sir John Betjemen and the Royal Fine Arts Commission. It received absolutely no support from the Mayor and several town councillors, who were more concerned with penny-pinching than heritage.

Eventually the Borough Council offered the building to the County Council, who accepted and commissioned their architect, Ralph Crowe, to restore and convert the building into a public library, arts and social centre.

The arts and social centre idea emanated from the Maltings Committee. This was a body of people who, in

1969, endeavoured to raise funds to purchase an old maltings at the top of the High Street for an arts and social centre. Having failed in their mission - thanks to the Borough Council - the Maltings Committee saw a heaven-sent opportunity in the Corn Exchange conversion and asked the County Council if space could be found for a small theatre, dressing rooms and a bar.

The County Council agreed and eventually the Corn Exchange reopened as a library and arts centre in June 1975. It was a scheme which was to be the pioneer for the whole of the country for the dual purpose of library and arts centre.

At the same time the Maltings Committee dissolved and the funds transferred to a new body with full charitable status - The Friends of Saffron Walden Corn Exchange.

The function of The Friends of Saffron Walden Corn Exchange is to underwrite musical and dramatic performances. They also arrange exhibitions, give what assistance they can to local amateur performers, help buy equipment and publicise activities, and also act as an advisory committee in the running of the Corn Exchange.

At the time the Corn Exchange was transformed into an arts centre and library, Area Librarian, John Shaw-Ridler also became Arts Director.

He says that when the Corn Exchange was offered to the County, with the idea of housing the library, it seemed, at that time, the building was too big for just a library, and he suggested that it be used for an arts centre as well, at the very same time that the Maltings Committee also put forward the idea.

John Shaw-Ridler came to Saffron Walden in 1960 as Area Librarian for the whole of Uttlesford District Libraries. At that time the County Library was housed in Cambridge House in Church Street, and occupied the whole of the premises apart from a tiny office and waiting room at the front of the building for the Registrar of Births, Marriages and Deaths. And, on the very top floor, in rooms which had once been dormitories when Cambridge House had been a school, there was a flat for the Librarian. (See Chapter Two - Church Street).

John Shaw-Ridler's "right hand man" is a woman, Mrs. Joy Marshall. It is she who is responsible for booking all the exhibitions, rehearsals, concerts, dramatic productions and craft fairs etc. She also does all the accounts and secretarial work for the arts centre as well as attending Private Views when held.

'Really,' she says, 'I am Jack-of-all-trades for the arts centre.'

'When we first started, we only had five or six bookings in the first three months, and now at peak times in the year, we might have as many as three events going on at the same time.'

Joy's husband - Harry - is also involved in the capacity of Treasurer of The Friends of the Corn Exchange.

Jill-of-all-trades at the library is Mrs. Jill Palmer, Deputy Area Librarian. Her duties, she insists, 'include everything - but mainly adult services.'

It is she who buys the book-stock for the adult library for the whole of the Uttlesford area and all the mobile libraries. She also runs services to homes for the elderly, where a selection of books is deposited every three months, as well as organising the Talking Book Service for the blind and partially sighted.

Senior Library Assistant Martyn Everett says his job is very "fragmented." Anything administrative falls into his province, which includes overseeing the cleaning and security of the building. He also deals with reader-enquiries and other general duties involved with the working of the library.

He says that most people do not realise how much work goes on at the library. 'Because we have the tourist centre, arts centre and library all under one roof, the Corn Exchange must be one of the most heavily used buildings in the town. It is used seven days a week, both during the day and in the evenings - we might have rehearsals for a play in the evening - and yet we still have to open-up as a library next morning. Sometimes, particularly in the Autumn we have three or four weeks so heavily booked we simply cannot slot people in.'

28

Martyn Everett is very much a local boy. Born in the town, educated first, at South Road School, then the Boys' British, later the County High.

He first came to the library during the 1970s, but left to become sub-librarian at Emmanuel College in Cambridge. After working for Emmanuel College for three years he did a three year B.A. joint Honours Degree in Sociology and History at Cambridge College of Arts and Technology. And then in 1983, rejoined Saffron Walden library as Senior Library Assistant.

Martyn is a fount of interesting statistics regarding the library. For instance during the 1986-7 year 266,051 books, cassettes and records were issued, and 4,700 requests were made for certain books. The total stock of books, which ranges from 14th and 15th century books to the latest Jeffrey Archer, is 56,347, including the mobile and village centre libraries.

'Not so long ago,' he said, 'we had a machine in the entrance lobby which actually recorded the number of people who were using the library. On a busy Saturday, we were getting 1,000 an hour coming in - and in fact - the machine broke down in the end.'

Another key member of the library staff is Janet Crofts. Janet's official title is - Librarian - Young and Education. This means that it is her responsibility to look after the children's side of the public library.

She also deals with all the primary schools in the Uttlesford area, visiting them once a term to promote books for the children, or help the teachers in working with books to use with the children for their topics.

Each school library has a minimum of 700 books from the County Schools' Library, and 150 of these may be exchanged each term. The Children's Library is also a mini-Resources Centre for the teachers.

Councillor and former Mayor, Viviane Barbour is one of the part-time members of staff who work on the counter of the adult library. She started working at the library shortly after the death of her first husband and when she re-married she continued with her work because she enjoys it so much.

It was the Friends of the Corn Exchange who realised - in 1978 - that there was a need for a Tourist Information Centre. Pressure on the library with queries about the town and overnight accommodation, had increased over the years. A group of individuals offered their services voluntarily and, together with a part-time paid employee, the Tourist Information Centre came into being.

First among the volunteers was Welsh-born Mrs. Mair Baxter who still works for the Tourist Information Centre.

Mrs. Baxter has lived in Walden since 1971 and speaks her native language fluently. This has stood her in good stead whilst working on the Tourist Information desk. Other volunteers manning the Centre come from other parts of Britain which, according to Mrs. Baxter, is extremely useful, because quite often they have enquiries about other parts of the country. And this means that usually at least one of them has some knowledge of the place in question.

The Tourist Information Centre is housed upstairs in the Reference Library at the Corn Exchange, and it is here, more often than not, you will also find Mrs. Elisabeth Blackie, the Tourist Information Officer.

Mrs. Blackie is Italian, married to an Englishman and has lived in this country for twenty years. Previously she worked for a travel agency in Rome - her native city - and as a hotel representative in New York. She says she loves meeting people and helping them, but dislikes "chaotic tourism". This she explains as people who, when they visit a place just wander around aimlessly not knowing quite where to go! And this is the reason why she took on the job!

She has a team of over 30 volunteers who help out at the Centre, and an accommodation list of about 75 different establishments in the area.

The Centre also has bus and rail time-tables - mostly for local people, plus books on accommodation all over the country as well as information on activities all over the country.

There are also lists of clubs and societies in the area which are regularly updated and checked. This is something particularly welcomed by newcomers to the district, as is the information pack sent to people thinking of coming to live in the district. The pack gives information on schools, doctors, dentists, estate agents etc. and a map of the town!

Since the Tourist Centre opened in 1978, it has grown enormously and Mrs. Blackie says that they are now finding that they do not have enough room. 'We are getting more enquiries, and the type of service which we offer is getting more sophisticated. Obviously we need more space.'

—— • ——

The actual history of Saffron Walden Library has been dealt with in Down Your Street Part One (pages 56-58). But as a library it is almost unique, in that it is really two libraries under one roof - the County Library and the Town Library, often referred to as The Victorian Studies Centre.

Someone who has watched the Town Library grow and flourish over the years is Mrs. Mary Whiteman who joined the library 50 years ago as an ordinary subscriber when she and her journalist husband came to live in the town.

Although she herself had grown-up in journalism, and still did a little part-time freelance journalism, she says she was mostly involved in bringing up her young family at that time. But she found the library fascinating, and became very friendly with the librarian Miss E.K. Wakeford.

'Miss Wakeford, was a scholar and a writer, with a deep appreciation of the contents of the original library. And it was through Miss Wakeford that I really got to know the library,' she says. 'As my children got older I became more and more interested, but it was not until the last five years of Miss Wakeford's time that I actually took an active part by becoming a member of the Books Committee.

When Miss Wakeford's health began to fail, I came in to give her a hand on a voluntary basis, until the last year of her life, when they actually paid me, 10 shillings (50p) a week, so that I would be a proper member of staff!

Miss Wakeford died very suddenly, so naturally I carried on. And by this time they were deciding the future of the library. We were suddenly rated for the first time and no longer regarded as a charity. This was also the time that the future of the Corn Exchange was being debated. So I held the fort until matters were resolved.

31

When the Town Library was taken over by the County Library - which was then at Cambridge House - I found myself on the counter of the County Lending Library, and my connection with the old books was severed for a time.

I was completely incompetent on the library counter, and perhaps, because they were glad to get rid of me, I went to work for Mr. Shaw-Ridler on the secretarial side. And so I was back with the old books once again. And by this time I realised the wealth of local history which we had and which needed to be developed.

My husband died in 1974, (he will be remembered by many people as the billeting officer during the second World War), and I must say, I found working at the library a tremendous help in enabling me to get over my bereavement.

When I retired in 1976, I found that I could now come into the library as an unpaid volunteer, and that was what I really wanted. And ever since then I have been involved with the Town Library.'

(Many people - myself included - have cause to feel grateful to Mary Whiteman and her interest in the "old books" as she calls them. Her knowledge of local history both inexhaustible and valuable.)

——— • ———

Leaving the library we cross the Market Place and come to the Town Hall, probably the ugliest building in this part of the town.

It was built in 1878-9, by George Stacey Gibson at his own expense, around an existing Town Hall dating back to 1761. The earlier building had replaced an even earlier Town Hall or Guildhall, believed to be similar to the one in Thaxted and probably dating back to the 15th century. It stood at the junction of King Street and the Market Place, and had five lean-to shops adjoining three sides, with a gaol on the ground floor and two rooms upstairs.

Alas the Georgians - like today's planning authorities - had scant regard for heritage. Justification for the demolition of the original building was, that it was in a poor condition.

The Town Hall 1761.

However 18th century architecture, unlike 20th century architecture, is seldom ugly, and the building which replaced the old Guildhall, although not exactly in keeping with a medieval market place, possessed a pleasing exterior, exhibiting all the spare elegance of the Georgian era. This was later completely spoiled by George Stacey Gibson's addition of a cumbersome mock-Tudor porch.

It was at this time also that Creepmouse Alley and Le Draperie, two of the Rows forming part of the old medieval market place were demolished.

Like its predecessor, the new Town Hall had a gaol on the ground floor. But this proved less than satisfactory, and there were many reports of prisoners in the gaol spitting on passers-by. This resulted in a new gaol being built at the top of the High Street in 1818 next door to the Workhouse (numbers 89 and 90 High Street).

The new gaol proved even less satisfactory than the old one and the Council was told that it would not be allowed to retain the Quarter Sessions - held in the town since 1657 - unless a suitable lock-up could be provided.

Eventually, after exploring various sites it was decided to purchase the house of Mr. Butterfield, the hairdresser, whose premises adjoined the Town Hall (now part of Nat-West Bank). And in 1841 the work on the new gaol was completed.

The Town Hall continued to serve as a police station and gaol until a purpose built police station was opened in East Street in 1886. (Down Your Street - part Two - pages 209-220). Nevertheless the cells in the Town Hall had to be retained for holding prisoners during their trials at the various Courts held in the building - the Borough and County Magistrates, the County Court and the Quarter Sessions.

In 1880 it was decided to appoint a Town Hall Keeper at a salary of £15 per annum. His duties included cleaning and dusting the various rooms - with the exception of the prisoners' cells which were the responsibility of the police - preparing and cleaning the Court; delivering notices of all meetings connected with the Corporation, and attending such meetings, as well as the letting of the various rooms in the building.

Mr. J.C. Crussell was the first Town Hall Keeper, a position he held until his death in 1893, when Mr. J.F. Penning was appointed. By this time the salary had been increased to £25 per annum plus an additional £7.10s for taking care of the Corn Exchange and an extra £15 for acting as market superintendent.

With the passing years the Town Hall became a great social centre (The Amalgamated Friendly Societies celebrated Queen Victoria's Diamond Jubilee in the Town Hall by holding a public dinner.) And by the 1930s dances and amateur theatricals were being performed regularly under its roof.

At the outbreak of the second World War, it became a reception centre for evacuees from London, with a billeting office on the second floor, and an Air Raid Wardens' post in the Town Hall Keeper's office. With the cessation of hostilities the building reverted to a more light-hearted role and once again it was a popular venue for local dances.

During the whole of its lifetime the shields on the front of the building had remained surprisingly blank until in 1957 it was suggested that they be blazoned with the arms of various people connected with the Borough of Saffron Walden. The Council agreed and the decorative work was carried out by the local sign writer Mr. A. Mitson.

' *Market Place 1920s showing "improved" Town Hall.*

The Arms - reading from left to right facing the Town Hall - are 1. Geoffrey de Mandeville; 2. Dame Johane Bradbury; 3. Humphrey de Bohun; 4. George Stacey Gibson; 5. Walden Abbey; 6. Sir Thomas Smyth and 7. Thomas Strachey.

The two premises flanking the Town Hall on either side have also played their part in the history of Saffron Walden. What is now part of the Nat-West Bank was once the hairdressing establishment of the Butterfield family.

I am not certain when Isaac Butterfield first opened his business at these premises, but his name appears in the rating lists for 1790 for this site. And, according to the rating lists, the premises remained in the Butterfield family for the next hundred years when the business was sold to a Mr. Burningham in 1892.

In the late 1920s it was owned by a Mrs. Windwood and

35

run by a Miss Walls whose great-niece Frieda Walls came to help her.

Young Frieda used to sleep over the shop, and a few years ago she told me what it was like to work in a hairdressing establishment in those days.

'It was a very old-fashioned establishment,' she said, 'we used to make toupees and all our own hair-dyes. They had to be freshly made every time you used them, and were hand mixed with a pestle and mortar. I remember doing the hair of a client from Stansted. She had beautiful auburn hair which she had coloured with the old-fashioned Egyptian Henna. Unfortunately I got the colour wrong, and she was extremely annoyed with me!'

But perhaps Frieda was not all that concerned at the client's outrage, she was probably more interested in a young man from Somerset who would ride his motor-bike round and round the market place. The young man's name was Maurice Hobbs. In due time he and Frieda were married, and they themselves founded another Walden family firm - Saffron Walden Motors. (Down Your Street - Part One - pages 30-31).

By the early 1930s Mrs. Windwood has sold her business to Mr. Pope, a gentlemen's hairdresser.

The following is an extract from a letter sent to me from Australia by Mr. William Glasscock who came to live in Saffron Walden with his widowed mother in 1934. Whilst still at the Boys' British School in East Street young William found himself an "out of school hours job" at Mr. Pope's hairdressing establishment. He writes:-

"They (the Popes) also had a good toy shop and sold fancy goods and cosmetics. I would start my work at 7.45 each morning until 8.45. The shop was opened by Miss Frieda Walls. The first job of all was to pick up The Daily Telegraph at Bloom's paper shop on the other side of the Town Hall.

The next job was to sweep the pavement, then polish the copper urn which heated the water for shaving over a gas burner. It took quite a lot of Brasso and much hard rubbing especially after the long opening hours of Saturday, which would be around twelve hours at a busy time. After this I would remove all the dust sheets covering the stock in the shop, fold them up neatly and put them away. Then, if it was Tuesday, (market day) many toys would be hung on hooks outside on the shop-front and piled on a plank under the window supported by two cardboard boxes. With this done I would go through the Rose & Crown yard to the Common and the Boys' British School.

Coming out of school at noon I would go to the shop to see if there were any parcels to deliver to customers. In those days if a customer spent four or five shillings in the shop they would expect their goods to be delivered home free of charge.

Back again to the shop at 4.45 to take out more parcels, if any, and take in the toys from the shop front and put them away. Most of these would be wooden horses, trucks and other wooden toys.

If it was winter-time it was my job to light the big gas lamps, one over each window. They were on the outside of the shop and shone into the window so as to clearly light it up. They had tiny pilot lights burning all the time and when a lever was pulled down with a hooked pole there was a "pop" and the lamp was lit. I believe the two sawn-off gas pipes are still there but the lamps have gone long ago.

After a few more jobs it would be 6.00pm, the shop would close and we would go home.

Saturday was the busiest day of the week. In addition to all the things I have mentioned, the front windows and door had to be cleaned and polished. Also at the back a large fluted mirror, hinged at the bottom and held at an angle by chains, had to be unhooked and cleaned. This was in a roofless area and when it rained the rain brought down dirt and grit, so it had to be thoroughly cleaned. The mirror reflected light into the men's saloon from the daylight above.

After this I would go down to the cellar and chop enough firewood to light the fire in the men's saloon for the next week. A few more odds and ends and it would be around 11.00 am and I would fetch buns for the morning break from Whites, in Market Hill. Mrs. Pope would treat us all and, for myself I would get a sticky "Chelsea Bun".

After we had all had a cup of tea and a bun Mrs. Pope would give me my wages: 2/6d (12^1/$_2$p). It sounds very small now but times were very hard and the Popes were kindly people."

The shop on the other side of the Town Hall, on the corner of Market Street and Market Place was originally owned by George Youngerman, Printer and Bookseller. His son, John Mallows Youngerman, was a wellknown landscape painter and etcher.

John Youngerman inherited his father's business and sold it to Boardman's of Bishop's Stortford, who traded at these premises for many years. Early on in the 20th century Mr. Bloom the printer had the premises and then later, it became Harts Bookshop.

Now it is a Woolshop, a business run for the past 10 years by Mr. and Mrs. Peter Maryon who lived in Walden for 16 years before moving to Bristol. One of their assistants is Mrs. Janet Schwarz who, despite her German name (she married a German prisoner of war who stayed on after hostilities had ceased) is very much a Walden girl.

Born in Castle Street, Mrs. Schwarz attended South Road School and later the Herts and Essex. Her father worked for Engelmann's Nursery, and when she left school she also went to work in the office at Engelmann's. When asked how she now came to be working in a woolshop, she replied, 'I was just a customer - and so I continued my hobby!'

———— • ————

Since Mr. J.C. Crussell was appointed first Town Hall Keeper for Saffron Walden Town Hall in 1880 he has had many successors, one of whom will still be remembered by a great many people - the late Mr. George Moore - who held the position for 30 years until he retired in 1965.

Mr. Moore was followed by Mr. Jim Manning, who took up his post in June 1966 and has only just recently retired.

Mr. Manning needs no introduction to anyone who has used the Town Hall for whatsoever purpose. And when he retired in December 1987 the Town Clerk's office was overwhelmed with letters of appreciation from grateful users of the building.

Before he came to Saffron Walden Jim Manning was a self-employed, fully qualified painter and decorator. But like all small businessmen, he experienced difficulty with people not paying their bills. And with a growing family of five children (including twin boys) he realised he must find work with more regular remuneration.

When his application for the position as Town Hall Keeper at Saffron Walden was accepted, he and wife, Olive, left their native Suffolk to take up residence in the town. It was an action which neither of them has ever regretted.

Since coming to Walden, Jim Manning has worked under five Town Clerks; eight Mayors and Two Councils - the old Borough Council and the present Town Council. 'And,' he says with all sincerity, 'in all cases I could not have worked for better people.'

In his early days as Town Hall Keeper the Corn Exchange, the Market and Town Hall, were the responsibility of the Borough Council, and came under his jurisdiction And at that time the Corn Exchange, despite declining business, was still functioning as a Corn Exchange.

'On Market Days it was my job to put out the desks for the Corn Merchants,' says Jim. 'There were about 12 or 14 desks, but we never had more than two or three Corn Merchants coming in to use them - certainly not more than six on the busiest days. But before my time, I believe it was very busy indeed.'

The Corn Exchange was also used for other functions - Jumble Sales and that sort of thing. Monday evening was Badminton evening. Unfortunately the glass roof leaked badly, and if it had rained during the day I would have to mop-up the floor, and get the Tortoise Stove going to dry it out, which meant that one end of the floor would be completely dry and the other still wet!

After the local Government reorganisation in 1974 Jim ceased to be accountable for the Corn Exchange. But he was still Market Supervisor, despite the fact that the District Council took away all the available labour for transporting the market stalls from the Pig Market where they were stored, to the Market Place. And he was still responsible for the letting and setting up of the stalls, as well as collecting the market tolls. (Tolls have been collected from stall-holders on Saffron Walden Market since the 16th century).

'Eventually,' he says, 'the stalls themselves got very much worse for wear, and it was decided to just let the spaces, and allow the traders to put up their own stalls, as had always been the case on Saturdays.'

But the letting and supervising of the Town Hall had always formed the bulk of Jim Manning's work. And in the days of the Borough Council this included preparing the Court Room for the Magistrates' Court - which at other times was used as a dressing room for the Operatic Society.

Sometimes a Special Court would be convened - 'and then,' says Jim, 'if the Operatic Society was performing at the same time - didn't we have fun and games! I would have to move all the costumes out of the dressing room to get the Court ready!

In my time,' he continues, 'I have seen three murderers brought to Special Courts in Saffron Walden.'

Saturday-night hops were also held in the Corn Exchange. 'We used to have local bands like The Ravens and all the youngsters would really enjoy themselves. And all the big firms would hire the Town Hall for their annual dinner dances. Sometimes a function would go on until one o'clock in the morning and then perhaps there would be a Court next morning!

But apart from the Courts and the special functions, there was also the preparation of the Council Chamber for meetings, and the laying out of robes and regalia for special occasions like Church Parades and Mayoral Processions. This in addition to making sure the building was clean from top to bottom, and showing people over the building.

Although I got Sundays off, there were times when I could be working seven days a week', says Jim. Small wonder then, that when he retired he confesses to having been 'completely lost' for the first four weeks!

But there aren't many people who can boast of having eight Mayors and Mayoresses at their leaving party. But that is what actually happened to Jim - all the former Mayors he had served under came along to give him a right-royal send-off!

41

CHAPTER TWO

Church Street

First published in the Saffron Walden Weekly News
September 28, 1989 – March 1, 1990

The origins of Church Street date from the first stone church built by the Normans in the 11th century and later replaced in the 15th century by the present building.

Like all the old streets in Saffron Walden, the fortunes of Church Street have waxed and waned throughout the centuries. But the 1851 Census List reveals that the inhabitants of 19th century Church Street were somewhat higher up in the social scale than their neighbours in nearby Castle Street, although both streets run parallel to each other and are connected by Museum Street.

Although Church Street had its share of working poor and artisans - butchers, bakers, grocers, laundresses, wheelwrights, and at least one straw bonnet maker - there was also a fair sprinkling of the professional classes, and at least two entries in the Census List under the heading of "landed proprietor".

The building standing on the south side of Church Street fronting the High Street - Cambridge House - has been dealt with in Parts One and Two of this series. But as the entrance to the Magistrate's Court - housed within - is in Church Street, perhaps a short resume of the history of Cambridge House will not go amiss:

It was built on the site of what was once one of the most important hostelries in the town - The White Hart. And it is said, that Samuel Pepys stabled his horse here on the 27th February 1660, the date he payed his historic visit to Audley End.

43

Unfortunately, the old inn was pulled down in the 19th century. Nevertheless it is believed that much of the original interior still remains.

Cambridge House was, for a short time in the 1960s and early 70s, the home of the Library, with the Librarian's flat above. Earlier still, during the second World War, many people will remember it as the British Restaurant.

Pupils of Cambridge House School 1877.

At the turn of the century however, it was a select "academy for young ladies" known as "Cambridge House School", established in 1860. By 1906 the school was run by the Cowell sisters, Rose and Laura.

Miss Kathleen Trigg and her sister Gladys, were boarders at the school between 1906 and 1908, as was their mother in 1877, when Mrs. Barrett was headmistress.

Recalling their schooldays at Cambridge House, Kathleen Trigg said that, 'the evenings at school were very pleasant for the boarders. We used to play cards and have informal dancing. Empire Day was celebrated by a holiday. This meant we could walk across the Park and go into Audley End Mansion, which was a great treat because it wasn't open to the public in those days.

On Saturday mornings, sometimes, Laura Cowell, would

44

get a shovel full of red hot cinders and pour neat carbolic acid over it, believing that the fumes would kill any germs on our clothes.

But things were rather different when I went back there to teach in 1916,' added Kathleen.

'By then the Miss Gowletts had taken over. The youngest, Miss Hannah, had been a pupil-teacher in our mother's day, now she was the housekeeper.

This was during the first World War, and Cambridge House was a very cold place. Often we had to wash in cold water, and although the maids were allowed hot water bottles, the teachers were not.

We were not even allowed to make ourselves hot drinks before going to bed at night. But we overcame this problem by secretly brewing ourselves hot drinks on a tiny stove in the teachers' Common Room. The Miss Gowletts would have had a fit if they'd ever found out.'

Later, Mollie, the youngest of the three Trigg sisters was to attend Cambridge House School. This was in the 1920s, and she sums up her memories of the School and the Miss Gowletts by saying 'it was not the happiest time of my life - alright if you were a favourite - but I never was!'

Towards the end of the late 1920s the Miss Gowletts moved their school from Cambridge House to a large house on Chaters Hill facing the Common - The Grove. Here, they remained, instilling "the best high principles" into the young ladies of Saffron Walden until 1938, when they finally retired. (Down Your Street - Part Two - pages 6-7).

——— • ———

Lift the latch on the gate of No.2 Church Street and you will find yourself in a small, pretty court yard. Take the flight of stairs to your left and they will lead you into a world of beauty - in more ways than one!

Lizzie's Health & Beauty Salon delights the eyes with a decor that is fresh and feminine without fussiness, and 21 year-old Lizzie herself is a charming advertisement for her enterprise.

Elizabeth Gooderham has been running her Beauty Salon

for just one year. And when asked why she chose a career in Beauty Culture she replied that she had always loved it. 'I've always had the knack of being able to pick up a brush and colour someone's face. So when I left school I trained at the London Institute of Beauty Culture.

After training, I worked at Sue Eatons at Limetree House for two years, and when I discovered they were closing down, I decided to capture the market and open up a salon here!'

Elizabeth Gooderham (centre) Sharon Poole (left) and Gaelle Curtis (right).

Lizzie certainly captured the market and over the past year she has increased her staff from a total of two (herself and an assistant) to three full time members of staff, plus herself and a trainee.

Although she is the sole proprietor of the salon, she stresses that all her family are very supportive (she has five sisters and one brother), particularly her mother who helped her to decorate and make the curtains for the salon.

Perhaps less by design and more by accident, Encore at No.2A Church Street compliments Lizzie's Beauty Salon.

Encore specialises in up-market nearly new clothes for discriminating women who love good quality clothes but cannot afford the initial outlay.

Mrs. Mavis Ashford, the proprietoress, told me she opened Encore seven years ago. 'It all started because I love good clothes, and I realised when I was talking to various friends that there were an awful lot of women like me, who appreciated really high quality clothes but could not afford to buy them.

Working in the shop is great fun, and I have the invaluable help of two assistants who enjoy it as much as I do. We meet some extremely interesting people, and sometimes it is more like a social occasion than a retail business.'

Next door to Encore is a large imposing building, built in Georgian style, and proudly proclaiming itself as "The Freemasons' Hall".

Porticoed and pillared, its numerous windows, glazed with frosted glass, reveal nothing. My vain hopes of peering through and finding at least one highly respected member of the community with his left breast bared and his right trouser leg rolled up and sporting a little leather apron, alas, came to nothing!

Strangely, despite its imposing appearance, the Freemasons' Hall was once a furniture repository for Robsons, the large retail emporium which flourished in King Street from about 1850 until the turn of the century. (Down Your Street - Part One - page 85).

Continuing along the street, we pass No.4, the house where Thomas Gatward the clockmaker lived when he first came to Walden with his father William Gatward in 1802. (Down Your Street - Part Two - page 163).

Now we come to No. 6 Church Street, a splendid house described in Department of Environment notes as an "18th Century red brick house, probably part of a former maltings - possibly the one at the rear of No.10 High Street (The Saffron Hotel)."

However, deeds belonging to No.6 (two of which are in Latin), translated and compiled by R.O. Denny of the College of Arms, London, go back to the early 17th century.

Long House, Church Street.

The first of these relates to Thomas Froswell, gentleman, of Audley End, who bought the house in 1624. Another dated 1703, describes the property as "Pages House" - probably the name of a former owner.

A brief history of the house, suggests that while the foundations and some of the walls date from an earlier house, the garden wall is undoubtedly of the Tudor period. And that the elevation on Church Street appears to have been rebuilt by the Wale family who were well-to-do booksellers in the City of London and owned the property from 1703 to 1741. In Regency times it was the house of a wig maker, and thereafter passed through several hands until it was bought by the late Lady Webb in 1953.

Lady Webb lived at No.6 - now known as "The Long House" from that date until 1971 when Mr. Richard Curry and his wife the late Mrs. Sheila Curry bought it.

The deeds of the house make fascinating reading. Often the house changed hands for just over £30 (remember we are speaking of the 17th and early 18th century). Frequently it featured as part of, or, the whole of the owner's Will. And not always was it the house of a rich man!

In 1844 Thomas Spurgin, General Practitioner, lived here, selling it in 1845 to Thomas Gayton, who describes himself as "landed proprietor" in the 1851 Census List. Gayton aged 43, was married to a young woman almost half his age - Mary Ann aged 26 - and had four children all under the age of five. Also living in the house at that time was a cook, a nurse, nursemaid and housemaid.

From about 1860 up until sometime in the 1890s, Gayton appears to have lived elsewhere, renting the property to a series of tenants. After the 1890s, rating lists show that the house changed hands quite often until Lady Webb bought it.

One great asset of No.6 Church Street is its delightfully secluded garden with its two vines. (One a cutting from a 300 year-old vine from Chicksands Priory - the other from Woolworths!)

David Campbell and his dog.

Next door and once part of the property - according to Department of Environment notes - is No.6A, the home of David Campbell the photographer.

49

David's photographs of Saffron Walden need no introduction to local people.

He is the son of the late John and Madge Campbell, born in Ashdon Road 68 years ago, and educated at the Grammar School.

David developed his love of photography at a very early age, and says he was quite tiny when he saw his first Box Brownie camera. It belonged to his uncle and a few years later he was actually allowed to use it!

He bought his very own first camera - a Kodak Hawkeye - by saving coupons from Nestle's chocolate bars! This, he says, must have been sometime in the 1930s.

After he left school, he became office boy at Emson Tanners, the wholesale grocers in the Market Place, gradually working his way up the ladder to become a clerk-typist. It was an ideal job for a budding freelance photographer because of the situation of the office. After all, most things in Walden happen in the Market Place! And David made sure he had his camera with him at all times.

By this time the second World War had started and film was hard to get. But David, whose camera was now a Leica,

Old Maltings, Church Street, demolished to make way for Barnards Court.

used 35mm offcuts from the film studies, and was thus able to keep up with his hobby.

Eventually he perfected his photography to the extent that he was able to sell photographs to the Weekly News and various magazines. And it was his success with the Weekly News which prompted him to give up his job after the war and turn professional freelance photographer.

Although David's father was Scottish, his mother, whose maiden name was New, was very much a local girl. Madge was a prominent member of the local Women's Institute, and will be remembered as a member of their Drama Group and also St. Mary's Players. She met her husband when he was stationed here during the first World War.

They moved to Church Street - first to part of the Sun Inn complex in the 1930s and to No.6A - the house where David still lives - in 1939. This was convenient for his father, who worked in the office of Cleales Motor Spares Department whose premises at that time were just across the road.

———— • ————

Barnards Court is a modern complex of town houses built on the site of a medieval cottage and a fine old malting. The cottage No.5 Church Street was demolished in 1957 'because it was very old and needed a lot doing to it!' and the malting at its rear was pulled down in 1974.

At the turn of the century Barnard Bros. corn and coal merchants were a household name in Saffron Walden. Their coal depots were all along the railway line between Saffron Walden and Bishop's Stortford, at the top of the High Street, and in the station yard itself.

The old malting in Church Street, approached through an archway in the High Street, was used by Barnards as a brewery for the beer they gave to their draymen. Later, as the need for coal declined, it was used as a grain drying store. (The archway, next door to Woolworths can still be seen and now leads to a small private car park.)

The demolition of No.5 Church Street left a valuable access to the malting, thus providing a site which could be developed for housing. And so it was that once again, Saffron Walden lost yet another part of its long history.

51

No.5 Church Street had been the home of Mr. Alfred Ketteridge and his wife, Georgina, since 1931. It was here that they brought up their family, one daughter and two sons - one of whom - now Councillor Jim Ketteridge - was to be elected Mayor of Saffron Walden in 1981.

Alfred Ketteridge, son of farmer, James Ketteridge, was born at Stocking Green Farm in 1903. (James, a tenant farmer, rented the property from Lord Baden-Powell).

But times were bad, and after 40 years working the same farm, James was forced to move. After working a succession of different farms, the Ketteridges ended up at a farm in Sewards End in 1921. Leaving one son to manage the farm, James Ketteridge took the rest of his family to live at No.11 Church Street.

By this time Alfred, their third son, as an employee of Raynhams in the High Street, was driving the mail van.

(In those days the Post Office never had vans of their own, and always hired them from Raynhams.) For ten years Alfred collected and delivered the mail to and from the railway station and round the local villages. And that was how he met Georgina who was in service at Ickleton.

Nos. 5 and 7 Church Street, demolished in 1956.

When they married they moved into No.5 Church Street, a very primitive cottage by today's standards (not unusual in the 1930s though). But No.5 had a wood yard behind it. So Alfred, who worked mostly nights, sawed up logs during the day and sold them for fuel. (Sunlighting instead of moonlighting perhaps?)

But by 1940, Alfred was tired of driving the mail van, also, the second World War was in progress, and he soon found himself employed by the Ministry of Agriculture to clear land for growing crops. His particular job was blasting out tree stumps, for which he had to have a gun-powder licence.

'In fact,' he says, 'I was the only person in Walden allowed to hold a licence for high-explosives during the war.'

When No.5 was deemed to be 'too old for modernisation', Alfred and Georgina moved to their present home - Catons Lane Farm - just beyond the football ground.

But a glance at old ratings lists reveals that this cottage, together with numbers 9 and 11 Church Street formed part of "Sparrow's Charity."

A paper written by local historian Mr. H.C. Stacey, to be found in the Town Library, states that "Joseph Sparrow of Saffron Walden (Town Clerk at the time of the William & Mary Charter of 1694) by Will dated 16th March, 1705, gave £5 for such honest and industrious poor of Saffron Walden, aged or overburdened with young children, or who shall accidentally meet with any other evident misfortune..."

It would appear that the rent from No.5, 9 and 11 and other property in Church Street was used, amongst other things, to finance apprenticeships for the sons of poor people.

Numbers 9 and 11, together with probably what was a third cottage, have all been made into one house, and called - appropriately - "Sparrows".

Sparrows is now the home of Mr. and Mrs. Philip Rees and their two children, Christopher (19) and Erica (16) and epitomizes old-world charm itself. Many-beamed with inglenooks it has been lovingly renovated by previous owners in 1981, who had the forethought to place a small plaque at the foot of one of the beams in the living room with the inscription "Sparrows Charity 1450."

Fortunately now listed, it is described in Department of Environment notes as "a 15th century timber-framed and plastered building, altered in the 17th and 18th or 19th century... Roofs tiled with a flat headed dormer to the lower wing and one gabled dormer with 17th century barge boards carved with guilloche ornamentation, above a cambered board carved in guilloche pattern, and with carved penants..."

Many people will recall however, that No.11 was once the home of Mrs. Mary Stayner.

Mrs. Stayner, once a professional actress, brought a highly professional touch to the local stage, as well as running drama classes for children in the Library.

But as a widow in her seventies, she stunned all her friends and acquaintances in the town by marrying a young man in his twenties. They ultimately went to live in Newport, where sadly she died a few years ago, after falling down stairs.

—— • ——

As we continue our way along the south side of Church Street we come to Harts Office Supplies. Those who have known Walden for a number of years will remember that Harts Office Supplies are situated on the site of Cleales Car Servicing Depot.

Harts Office Supplies is a Branch of Harts Booksellers in King Street, run by two directors, 36 year-old Martin Turnbull and his 26 year-old brother, Andrew.

The story of Henry Hart the young printer who, at the age of 35, set up business in King Street in 1836 has been dealt with fairly extensively in Parts One (pages 64-70) and Two (pages 67-71) of this series.

But Harts Office Supplies is a far cry from the business young Henry Hart founded over a hundred years ago. In those days typewriters had not been invented. So what he would have thought of all the advanced office technology on display at Harts goodness knows.

So sophisticated has office technology become that now, in 1989, Harts no longer stock manual typewriters! Word-processors and electronic typewriters - yes - but the old click and rattle machines with their ting, ting bells are now a thing of the past in a modern office.

Harts also opened yet another branch of their company - Aimprint - nine years ago. This is run by Miss Eve Piechocki and her three assistants at No.29 Church Street. Aimprint was set up in response to the many requests that Harts had from customers for printed business forms and other company stationery.

Now they offer a complete printing service right through, which includes design of all company stationery requirements from a simple business card to a full colour brochure.

Mr. Coe the blacksmith standing outside his forge – late 1890s – now the site of Aimprint.

Aimprint of course, as many people will recall stands on the site of Cleales tractor sales depot, and this particular site, is also believed to have once been the forge of Mr. Coe the blacksmith.

Also, many people will remember Cro's Stores, which once flourished in the High Street, and moved to No.15 Church Street, later to become a sports outfitters called Highdays. When Highdays became vacant a few years ago the building was also incorporated into Harts Office Supplies.

———— • ————

Skingle House, from the early 1950s until 1982, was also part of Cleales Motor Engineers. Before that it appears to have been a private house. That is, apart from a few years during the second World War when it was commandeered by the Military Authorities.

Department of Environment notes describe it as "an early 19th century red brick house - now painted."

For most of its long life it appears to have always been known as "No.17 Church Street", until a few years ago when Skingle Smith, Major & Major, chartered accountants,

Skingle House 1989.

56

had their offices on the top floors. The building was then named Skingle House - after the senior partner - Edward Skingle Smith.

But since 1985 these offices have been occupied by another firm of chartered accountants - Peters Elworthy & Moore – and it was here that I met Mr. Bill Wilsdon. He told me that Peters Elworthy & Moore were founded in Cambridge in 1875, and opened up a branch office in Market Street, Saffron Walden, in 1935.

Mr. Wilsdon, will be well known to many businessmen in the Walden area, especially local farmers. He and his staff of nine accountants number a great many of them amongst their long-standing clients.

He pointed out that, although they are a very old-established company, there is nothing old-fashioned about the way they handle clients' business.

Downstairs, Skingle House is divided into two – on one side is the Church Street Gallery – and on the other – The Reproduction Folio.

The Church Street Gallery is owned and run by Mrs. Patricia Pickard who opened in Church Street six years ago.

She displays only the work of professional artists, and specialises in watercolours with a small section given over to 19th century oils.

Amongst the water-colours on show at the Gallery is Annie May Youngman's "Flowers in a Vase". Annie May Youngman was born in Saffron Walden in 1859, the daughter of John Mallows Youngman, landscape painter, (whose father, George Youngman, Printer and Bookseller of Saffron Walden had a young apprentice named Henry Hart!)

At Reproduction Folio next door, Barry Evans sits surrounded by handsome Regency and Georgian furniture.

It is true the pieces on show are all replicas, but they are authentic in every detail, executed with expertise and craftsmanship.

Forty year-old Barry Evans and his partner 28 year-old Matthew Leopold, have been running their reproduction furniture business for just over four years. Recently they

Journalist, Mary Whiteman and local artist Anna Brooker in the garden which replaced Dorset House.

have been joined by their wives - Beryl and Jackie - all four are partners. Beryl - Barry's wife - helps in the shop, and Jackie - does the books.

When The Reproduction Folio first came into being, Barry and Matthew, sold their furniture from a brochure, and sold mainly to the Trade. That is why they now call themselves The Reproduction Folio.

Barry admits that when they first started out he didn't know a thing about furniture.

'I ploughed all my savings into the business and literally took a crash course in the furniture trade. It was different for Matthew; he had been in the furniture business all his life. But reproduction furniture is not like antique furniture, you do not have to know your history, and as long as you know the product you are selling reasonably well - you are alright!'

However, they have come a long way since those early days when Barry was the only one who could afford to work full time, and Matthew had to keep on with his own job, helping out evenings and weekends. Now Matthew has come into the business as well as Beryl and Jackie and recently they have found it necessary to employ 16 year-old Ian Payne as well.

It's still a 7 day a week job though, according to Barry, and when the doors close at 5.30, more often than not, they are down at the warehouse in Clavering or out delivering furniture. And as well as selling high quality reproduction furniture, they also repair and re-polish existing furniture for their customers.

—— • ——

Across the road from Skingle House is a small row of picturesque 15th and 16th century cottages known as Church Path, which lead directly to the southern approach of the Church. The tiny garden facing Church Path is all that is left of a building known as Dorset House.

When Dorset House was demolished in 1957, many felt that its removal opened up a whole new vista of the church

59

Dorset House.

as well as providing a pleasant green space to sit and quietly contemplate the time-enduring qualities of Saffron Walden.

Alas, perhaps the wealthy man who built Dorset House felt he also was creating something with time-enduring qualities. Early photographs of this building depict it as a large, three storey dwelling with attics, a hipped roof and a Georgian façade, with a smaller - probably older - cottage adjoining.

Unfortunately records do not reveal when it was actually built and its history can only be traced back to 1790 when it was the home of George Archer. Later, according to the 1851 Census List, it appears to have been a school run by Benjamin Taylor aged 24, his wife Catherine (26) and three other teachers.

In 1868 it was purchased by Joseph Bell - the builder -from Joseph Collin, the solicitor who practised in Church Street.

Joseph Bell was to live at Dorset House for the rest of his life until he died in December 1911.

As a specialist in restoring old churches and large country houses, Joseph Bell employed many local men. He himself, was a prominent member of the community, and served as Mayor of Saffron Walden no less than 10 times.

After his death the house belonged to his daughters, Edith and Lucy, but never used as a private dwelling. Strangely, old ratings lists indicate that, in 1920, part of it was rented by the governors of the Grammar School for a schoolroom.

Mr. John Wiseman of Herberts Farm Wimbish clearly remembers this phase in the history of Dorset House because he commenced his education at Saffron Walden Grammar School in September 1920. And for a very short time, his class had their lessons in Dorset House.

He writes:- "I think it (Dorset House) must have closed as a school a few months later. At seven years of age I cycled daily from Wimbish (four miles), but soon became a weekly boarder, and was usually taken and fetched home by my sister in a pony and trap or the Model T. Ford.

At that time "Bertie" Parrack was Headmaster. The only other teacher I can remember was the Rev. Doble, vicar of Great Chesterford. He arrived at the school on his motor bike with sidecar attached, and I have memories of him on his motor bike wearing a brown tribly hat with the rim turned up at the front.

At the school we had three dormitories each named after an illustrious old boy - Winstanley of the lighthouse fame - Harvey - circulation of the blood - and Mellish - the first V.C. in World War one."

At the same time it was being used by the Grammar School, Dorset House was also also rented by the Essex War Pensions Committee, and the newly inaugurated Comrades Club. And then, from the thirties onwards, it housed the Public Assistance Committee and the Territorial Association.

Whilst the demolition of the old house has provided us with an interesting and attractive view of the church, it is sad to think that yet another episode in the history of Saffron Walden has been wiped out.

Someone, however, who took advantage of the tiny garden which replaced Dorset House, and who, in turn, has contributed in some measure to recording the history of the town, is Ian Miller, Managing Director of the publishing company C.W. Daniel.

En route to Cambridge on a lovely June day in 1978, the Miller family - Ian, his wife Jane and their two children

Genevieve and Barnaby - broke their journey to watch the Morris Men dancing in Saffron Walden. Whilst the rest of the family watched the dancing Ian wandered around the town, and sat for a while on one of the seats in the garden opposite the cottages in Church Path.

It was then that he saw that No.1 Church Path was up for sale. It so happened that the object of the Millers' journey to Cambridge was to look for new premises for their London based publishing company. And it then occurred to him that Saffron Walden would do just as well as Cambridge, and he promptly made an offer for the cottage.

It took the Millers a year to renovate No.1, and to find a home to live in nearby. Since when, The C.W. Daniel Company Ltd. has become very much a part of the Saffron Walden scene. Although they consider themselves "New Age" publishers and specialise in books on alternative healing, they have also been responsible for three books on Walden. (H.C. Stacey's "Saffron Walden in old photographs", Mary Whiteman's and Anna Brooker's "Saffron Walden Portrait of a Market Town", and "Saffron Walden a Pictorial Guide" - photographs by Peter Wigley and text by Rosanne Kirkpatrick.)

Ian, who has been in publishing right from the time he left school, married a printer's daughter. And it was his father-in-law who drew his attention to an almost defunct publishing house called C.W. Daniel, which, in the early 1970s, was run entirely by two old ladies.

Charles William Daniel, 1871 - 1955, had been born very much before his time. He was a friend of Tolstoy, and during the first World War was imprisoned for publishing anti-war literature.

He also published the very first book on homosexuality in this country. It was called "Despised and Rejected", and was immediately seized as soon as it was published, and Daniel himself brought to Court. Fortunately, a fellow publisher - who had really been responsible for persuading Daniel to publish the book in the first place, felt so guilty that he organised a whip-round amongst other publishers, which paid his fine, and also left enough money for Daniel to continue publishing.

One of the old ladies running the company was a spiritualist and said that she felt Ian had been sent by the spirit of Charles William Daniel. But Ian pointed out to both of them that although he would love to buy the firm, he did not have enough money, to which they replied 'money is not important!'

So Ian - who in his youth had been employed by all the major publishing houses and had reached the stage - so he says - of being virtually unemployable - bought the company for £700 and became a publisher in his own right.

'Most of the titles were incredible,' he says. 'They were on all sorts of subjects. But amongst them was one on the Bach Flower Remedies, another on colour healing and a third on The Gospel of Peace of Jesus Christ, and they were really the basis of our list and we have worked our way up from there.

The books had been down in the cellar for years, and when we first started to sell them an American bookseller asked us - 'how do you get your books to smell so organic?'.

Now Ian and Jane (who is also a director of the Company) have 250 titles on their list; exhibit at the Frankfurt Book Fair every year, as well as the American Book Fair and even the Tokyo Book Fair - and are 'incredibly international!'

Mrs. Sylvia Carter lives in the last cottage in Church Path which overlooks the churchyard. And it is thanks to Mrs. Carter that the churchyard of St. Marys is as neat and tidy as it is, because she has made it her personal responsibility to look after it.

She says, 'I told the town clerk that I didn't want to be a paid council worker, I wanted to work when I pleased. And I think I have saved the rate-payers hundreds of pounds during the time I have been looking after the churchyard.

'There is always something to do here all the year round, except perhaps January and February. I love being out here in the fresh air. I have all my birds - there is a Robin who follows me around - and there are lots of squirrels, and then there is Owlie! He's a gorgeous owl who hoots in the daytime. I have only actually seen him once, but I hear him frequently.'

Sylvia Carter (née Burleigh), a farmer's daughter, was born at Great Chesterford, 72 years ago, in a house -

63

Carmelstead - which her family had lived in for 200 years. And five generations of them, including her own sons, attended the Saffron Walden Grammar School (now Dame Bradburys).

She has been familiar with the town all her life, and one of her earliest memories is, of coming into Walden in a pony and trap driven by her mother. So when she moved into No.4 Church Path 21 years ago, she said it was as if she was coming home.

But someone who remembers No.4 Church Path long before Mrs. Carter made it her home, is retired Squadron leader R.E. Leach M.B.E., B.A., who lived in the cottage with his mother and grandmother - Mrs. Helen Holland - from 1940 until June 1945.

He writes:- "Thereafter, we returned to the family home at Wimbledon to rejoin my father, who had visited us once a month throughout the war. I never really settled down in Wimbledon and took every opportunity, such as school holidays, half terms etc. to return to Saffron Walden and my friends, some of whom still live there.

As children do, I had my own close friends and, on reflection, seemed to go through an annual cycle of activities that had no formal start date, but just seemed to occur at about the same time each year. There was snowdrop and violet picking, the May Day garland collections of Pagals (cowslips to the uninitiated), birds nesting (alas no longer the thing to do, with good reason) sloe picking (can't think what granny used to do with them!!) rabbiting at harvest time, damming the Slade when it was in spate, skating on the New Pond without skates and other pastimes too numerous to mention. Many of my "gang" were members of the St. Mary's Church choir as well as regular attendees at the Castle Street Sunday School.

During the war, we became great friends with an Army officer, Colonel "Jock" Kennedy, who commanded the SOE training school at Audley End Mansion. He used to take us to watch the "foreigners" firing, throwing grenades, driving lorries over an obstacle course and some such. He had been a regular Army officer before the war, retiring to a headmastership in his homeland of Scotland. He was recalled on the outbreak of war and became a great friend to numerous Saffron Walden children.

Among our playing areas were Gibson's Estate, complete with walled garden, pond, well and the summer house on the mound. Other places included "the hilly bumps", the paddling pool, battle ditches, Butney Barn, Fry's and Jubilee Gardens, Beechey Rye, Audley End Mansion grounds and the railway station (train spotting)."

We leave No.4 Church Path with its happy memories to take a walk in the churchyard. Unfortunately most of the gravestones have been moved and placed around the walls, and those that are still in position are so timeworn it is difficult to read the inscriptions. All that is, with the exception of Lord "Rab" Butler's grave in the north-east corner. No-matter what the season, this is always extremely well-tended.

The Verger's Cottage is also worthy of attention. This is described by the Department of Environment as "the surviving crosswing probably of an early 16th century timber-framed and plastered house with timber-framing exposed. (The remainder of the house, now the parish rooms was rebuilt in the late 19th century)".

Before we visit the church itself, let us take a look at the Rectory. A few years ago, the future of this splendid Georgian building, looked very doubtful indeed. (Down Your Street - Part One - page 224).

At that time (1985) it was still functioning as a home for the Rector of St. Mary's, but its days as such, were numbered. Plans were afoot to demolish the Rectory and build houses in its garden. Fortunately there were enough far-sighted and caring people in the town to put up a fight to save this architecturally and historically interesting building.

Now, four years later, the Rectory - enlarged - but still architecturally pleasing, stands, performing - perhaps an even more vital role in the life of the community than it ever did before - offering a combination of both physical and pastoral welfare.

Two years ago "The Rectory Practice" came into being when Dr. Burton Chalmers, Dr. Philip Sills and Dr. Andrew

The Rectory 1958.

Smith moved their Practice from No.67 High Street to the Rectory. Since when they have been joined by two more General Practitioners, Dr. Clive Paul and Dr. Jane Weir.

According to Dr. Smith, a previous Rectory had once stood on this site. This fact being borne out by a Latin-inscribed plaque on the northern wall of the house - which had fallen down.

This information co-incides with an entry in Colville's "English Architects 1660-1840". The entry states that the present building was designed and built by William Ivory, 1747-1837, carpenter and builder of Saffron Walden, who carried out works at Audley End for Lord Howard de Walden, which included repairs to the House and a new Vicarage in Saffron Walden, erected in 1793.

Despite his noble patron, William Ivory does not appear to have died a rich man. He ended his years in the Edward

VI Almshouses at the age of 90, and now lies, close to the house he built, in the churchyard of St. Mary's.

Had he been alive today, surely he would have been pleased with the work of his modern-day counterpart - architect Brian Christian, of Great Chesterford - whose design for the Old Rectory has won an award for the best conversion of a listed building and the best extension to a listed building.

Certainly all who work within the Practice feel that Brian Christian's sympathetic treatment of the existing rooms, and his willingness to become involved and listen, has resulted in a scheme which really works.

To augment the historical associations of the building Dr. Chalmers thought of putting up a tablet - now in the course of preparation by Latin scholars at Cambridge University - which will read "Where the Rector once cared for people's souls, now doctors look after their bodies as well."

Just before the Practice moved into the Old Rectory, an Open Morning was held with an invitation to patients to come along. Many of them were no strangers to the place and several recounted their memories of attending Confirmation Classes held in what is now the waiting room. One patient pointed out one of the sash-windows in the room, saying he had worked on it as an apprentice-joiner, and believed that it was one of the first sash-windows in Walden.

When asked how they felt a Group Practice compared with the old-fashioned single-handed family doctor's Practice, Dr. Paul said that a Group Practice is much better for the doctor. A single-handed doctor is on call all the time, whereas with a group the work-load is shared out. But at the same time a small Group Practice with just three or four doctors means that the doctors get to know all their patients.

Dr. Smith felt the Rectory Practice was just the right size and that when he was on duty at weekends he always knew the person at the other end of the 'phone as well as the family itself.

Both doctors stressed the importance of getting to know their patients well, and felt that the surroundings helped enormously with their job satisfaction. 'If you have job satisfaction it certainly helps to give a better service to your patients.'

On the touchy subject of the proposed changes in the National Health Service, it was very clear that both Dr. Smith and Dr. Paul felt very strongly about them. Dr. Smith summed things up by saying, 'if we are just to be driven by market forces instead of our genuine wish to look after people it would be a shame!'

No-one can doubt the genuinely friendly and happy atmosphere at The Rectory Practice and this was echoed in no small way by Mrs. Vera Thompson.

Vera Thompson needs no introduction to those who were former patients at the Practice of Dr. Justinian Bartlett and Dr. Chalmers, where she worked as receptionist 20 years ago. When Dr. Bartlett retired, Mrs. Thompson accompanied Dr. Chalmers on his move to No.67 High Street to join Dr. Gladys Gray's Practice. Since when she has seen the Practice grow, from two doctors to five, and 'eight or more' receptionists.

When the Practice moved, again, she moved also, and when, shortly before her retirement she was offered the converted coach house of the Old Rectory for her retirement home, she was thrilled to bits.

'The nice thing was,' she said, 'they offered it to me, I think it was extremely kind of them and I shall never be able to thank them enough!'

It is not surprising that Mrs. Thompson loves living in her coach house, it must surely be one of the most delightful small cottages in Saffron Walden, and this year was entered for a similar design award as the Rectory itself.

She admits that when she first saw the cottage she did not think it could be made into a house because it was only one storey, and she still remembers the pile of hay that once stood in a corner of what is now her sitting room. But now she has a large and compact kitchen-diner, delightful sitting room, two bedrooms, and bathroom.

Mrs. Thompson was born in Little Walden, and her father was Mr. Maskell the Dairyman of Thaxted Road. Shortly after her marriage she left Walden, but returned after the second World War.

Certainly the Rectory has undergone a happy transformation, what I wonder what would the Rev. Ralph Clutton have thought about it all? Could he envisage, when he lived there in 1851 with his wife Isabella, their four children, and four servants (nurse, cook, housemaid and nurserymaid) that one day his large house would play a completely different, but no less important, role in the lives of the people of Saffron Walden?

——— • ———

A great deal has been written about Saffron Walden Parish Church, so its history will only be briefly touched upon here. Those interested in learning more will find helpful booklets in the church itself.

St. Mary the Virgin c.1450 is claimed to be the largest church in Essex, with an overall length of 183 feet, and height (tower and spire) of 193 feet and stands on the site of an earlier, 12th century stone church.

John Wastall, premier stone-mason of the mid 15th century - builder of the central tower of Canterbury Cathedral - was the stone-mason engaged to carry-out the building of the church. The financial responsibility being shouldered, in the main, by John Leche, incumbent at that time, and his sister, Dame Joane Bradbury, widow of a Lord Mayor of London. They also received some support from various influential people, including King Henry VIII who gave a hundred oaks from the Forest of Chesterford.

During the Civil War the church provided a meeting place for Cromwell and General Fairfax during a time of discontent amongst the soldiers. But there is no evidence whatsoever to support the popular story that Cromwell's men used the church as a stable and mess-room.

Severe structural damage occurred to the building when it was struck by lightning in 1769, and during the twenty years that followed, the fabric deteriorated considerably through general neglect.

In 1790 however, restoration work was put in hand which unfortunately removed most of the church's medieval features. Later, in 1830, it was decided to replace the curious wooden steeple, said to have been designed by Henry Winstanley (designer of the first Eddystone lighthouse) by the present, more elegant, slightly crooked, spire.

The vicar's appeal to the community for contributions for the replacement of the original steeple was well received by all except Wyatt George Gibson, (a member of the notable Quaker family) who refused, but later consented to donate £300 to have the old spire pulled down. Strangely enough, it was another Quaker, Thomas Rickman, who designed the new spire.

Of course in those days the churchyard woud have looked rather different from what it does now. It would have been surrounded by iron railings for one thing, (removed during the second World War) and Dorset House would have concealed quite a bit of the southern aspect of the church.

The bells of St. Mary's are said to be one of the largest rings in Essex. Eight of them were cast in 1798 from the metal of a previous peal, and four others added in 1914. Also worthy of note - the Saffron Walden Society of Change Ringers is over 300 years old, and one of the oldest in the country!

A few years ago it was decided to restore the custom of Great Ringing Day, which dates back to 1642. The story behind this - so it is said - is of a stranger who got lost in a nearby forest one day. And who, by following the sound of the bells of St. Mary's, eventually found his way out of the forest. In gratitude to the bells and their ringers, he left money in his Will for the bells to be rung all day long one day every year thereafter.

This story was related by a lady who lived all her life within earshot of the bells. She also added, that her father always made a point of taking the whole family away for an outing on Great Bell Ringing Day!

Although there are many monuments to various wellknown dignitaries of the town in the church, including the Banner Of The Most Noble Order of The Garter, which belonged to the late Lord Butler. (To be found hanging at the west end of the nave). And the marble tomb of John Leche himself in the north chapel, the memorial brass to Charlie Luckings appears to be missing.

70

This is very strange because when he died almost 20 years ago at the age of 90, he had been verger of St. Mary's for more than 10 years and a memorial brass in his memory was said to have been erected.

He was born in 1880, and as a child was sent to the workhouse. But at the age of 15 went to sea as a cabin boy on one of the old windjammers. Later he worked on a sea-going barge carrying pitch to Dunkirk.

He had two marriages, both happy, and celebrated two silver weddings. (His first wife died in 1937, and he remarried in 1939). And for many years lived at No.87 Castle Street (now demolished).

A well-known local character, Mr. Luckings was a coalman for 34 years and a founder member of the Gate Bowls Club.

As verger he was a familiar sight in the churchyard, mowing the grass with his hand mower, and it would be nice to think that there is a memorial brass to Charlie Luckings somewhere in the church. Surely a former workhouse boy has a right to take his place amongst those more nobly born? After all his contribution to the history of the church was no less than theirs.

—— • ——

Joseph Thomas Collin, solicitor, rented No.16 Church Street from his father, the Rector of Quendon on the 5th January 1834. The very next day, the 6th January, his father gave him the freehold of the property, and from that day onwards, No.16 and the adjacent No.14 have always been associated with the practising of Law.

Joseph Collin, following the family tradition, qualified for the Law in 1831. His grandfather John Collin, had practised in Saffron Walden for many years, probably from Dorset House. Joseph, it is believed, was first articled to an uncle in Dunmow. Evidence to support this theory lies in the fact that a solicitor by the name of Collin practised in Dunmow in the 18th century.

In the early days Joseph both lived and worked at No.16, but around about 1850 he moved to Dorset House, and then Mutlow Hall, Wendens Ambo, which he inherited on the

71

Turner Collin and family on the Tennis Court of No. 16 Church Street – 1898.

death of his father. His daughters, however continued to live at No.16, whilst the adjoining house, No.14, became the office. And many years later, in the early 1960s, part of the ground floor of No.16 was re-numbered as No.18 Church Street.

As a practising solicitor in a small market town, Joseph Collin held many appointments - Clerkships to the Magistrates of Saffron Walden and Linton, to the Commissioners of Taxes Saffron Walden and Linton and the Linton Guardians. He was also Registrar of the Saffron Walden County Court and a Trustee of the Almshouses and Amalgamated Charities, all appointments which continued to be held by his successors throughout the years that followed.

Turner Collin, Joseph's son, born at Dorset House in 1852, also qualified as a solicitor and became his father's partner in 1877. The original manuscript partnership agreement is still in existence and states that Turner was required to purchase a horse "always to be ready for office work."

On his father's death in 1888 Turner took over all his

father's appointments, and it was during his time as Clerk to the Magistrates of Saffron Walden, that the hearing of the infamous Moat Farm murder was held in the Town Hall in 1903.

In 1895 Turner Collin was joined by a Lincolnshire man, William Adams, who had arrived in Saffron Walden in 1886. It was then that the name of the firm changed from "Jos. Thos. & Turner Collin" to "Collin & Adams".

Three years later, in 1898, Edmund Charles Frank Land became clerk to Turner Collin, qualifying as a solicitor in 1920 and partner in 1929 on the retirement of Turner Collin. Again the name of the firm was changed, this time to "Adams & Land".

The name "Adams & Land" was to survive for the next 60 years, until October of this year when it became "Adams & Harrison" after amalgamation with Harrisons of Haverhill.

This information was given to me by the senior partner of Adams & Harrison, Mr. Tony Watson, who joined the firm in 1952 as office boy.

But things have changed a good deal in solicitor's offices since those early days of Mr. Watson's career. And he gave as an example one of the numerous menial tasks, as office boy, he had to perform. This was to turn on the lights of the partners' and managing clerk's cars as dusk fell during the winter evenings. He was speaking of course, of the halcyon days when motorists could park mostly wherever they chose!

Those were the days when the deed of a large farm purchase would be sent up to London to be hand-written, when a typing error on a legal document meant a complete re-type, and every single plan had to be hand drawn, with every additional copy traced.

Now with the ultimate sophistication of modern office technology, a staff of 12 people - four "fee" earners (people working directly for clients) and eight support staff, Adams & Harrison cope with four times the volume of work done by 18 members of staff in the 1950s.

This, Mr. Watson said, has meant a corresponding reduction in fees, he quoted as an example, a house on a Thaxted Road housing estate which was sold for £4,000 and

73

for which they charged a fee of £40. Ten years later the same house was sold for £40,000, and this time their fees were £200.

Like all young men of his age Mr. Watson had to do his National Service which meant serving in the R.A.F. as a regular in Cyprus during the Suez Crisis of 1956. Afterwards he returned to Adams & Land to take his Articles and was ultimately made a partner in 1965.

His father, Ernest Frank Watson, a second cousin of Edmund Charles Frank Land, had joined the firm in 1943 and had been made a partner in 1946. He died in 1975, six months before he was due to retire, and like his predecessors held many and varied appointments in the town.

Unlike his father, Tony Watson does not hold quite so many appointments apart from being current Chairman of the Citizens Advice Bureau Management Committee, and Vice-Chairman of the Museum Society. The latter appointment being a connection the firm has held for many years. William Adams had been President of the Museum Society when the Museum was 100 years old, and Joseph Thomas Collin was one of the founder members of the original Natural History Society, later to become the Museum in 1835.

(In their heyday, the Gibson family had all been clients of the firm, and there is still a limited connection with them because of the administration of a trust set up by George Stacey Gibson.)

Although No.14 and the adjoining property, No.16 Church Street, is very much a solicitor's office, with portraits of past senior members lining the walls ascending the stairs, there is a unique and quite charming piece of history which, during some minor alterations a few years ago, was accidently uncovered.

This consists of three doors, in what had obviously been a nursery, completely covered in Victorian cutouts. They reveal a montage of social comment on the world of the Victorian child, and are attributed to Beatrice Maud Pearson, daughter of Turner Collin, whose granddaughters Misses Sylvia and Esme Pearson are now ladies in their seventies.

Turner Collin also had a son believed to have been killed in the Boer War.

Part of No.18 Church Street is now given over to the Citizens Advice Bureau, a valuable service set up at the outbreak of the second World War, to give free, confidential advice to people in need of help.

In those days there were few suitable premises, and air-raid shelters, rest centres and village halls were frequently used as offices. Converted horse boxes were also used as mobile offices to visit badly bombed areas where transport was difficult.

Early days for the Citizens' Advice Bureau.

Later, custom-built mobile units came into use, and many people in Saffron Walden must remember seeing the CAB van parked in the Market Place on Friday mornings. At that time the service provided for the town was an extension of the Braintree Bureau, and two people who worked for the CAB in those early days were Dorothy Mennie and Vivian Bolam. Recalling their memories of those days in the Bureau's Annual Report for 1988/89, they write:-

"There was no telephone in the van, nowhere to shelter from the rain, and those who did attend often scuttled up the ramp hoping to be unobserved.

We sat behind drawn curtains, knee-to-knee, with warm air hissing from the calor gas tank suspended beneath the floor. Breathing became uncomfortable and eyes stung, so usually we worked without heat in the winter. Often, when we were busy, clients were interviewed in the driver's seat!"

In 1977 the Bureau moved into the Library, and then in November 1983, moved to its present address. This was when it was decided to set up an independent Bureau for Saffron Walden, and Mrs. Sylvia Lowe became the Bureau's first part-time manager.

Mrs. Lowe, who holds a degree in Law, lives in Great Chesterford and has worked for the CAB since 1980. She became involved because she was actively concerned with both the Women's Institute in Cambridge and the Federation of Women's Institutes.

'From time to time a member of the Executive Committee was represented on the Cambridge Committee of the CAB, and that is how I heard about it and I thought it sounded interesting. So I volunteered.'

When asked what type of person volunteered to work for the CAB, Mrs. Lowe replied, 'they must be sympathetic, tolerant and understanding people, with a lively, intelligent mind. But,' she added, 'it is not necessary to have formal qualifications. We are always on the lookout for volunteers, and I would particularly like to get more men volunteers.'

'Training necessitates working in the Bureau for the first eight weeks, learning about the information system and sitting in on interviews. This is followed by attending a training session at Chelmsford for one day a week for nine weeks, after which the trainee returns to the Bureau to work for a time under supervision. Six months later there is a further three days of what is called "basic call-back", followed by another four or five days of intermediate training a year later, after which the trainee is a fully fledged adviser.'

Despite the amount of training, and the essential commitment of the work (everyone has to do a minimum of six hours a week at the Bureau on a regular basis, plus "Advisers Meetings" once a month, which includes some aspect of training) Mrs. Lowe said they have very few dropouts. Although she did admit that some volunteers do find that the work isn't quite what they thought it was.

She also pointed out that the CAB does not train people over the age of 65, and at the moment the retirement age for volunteers is 70.

Speaking of the changes in clients' problems during the nine years she had been working for the CAB, she said that debt cases had increased. She had thought Social Security was the main problem when she first started, but with the high interest rates now, the number of re-possessions has gone up, and a lot of people were having to rent out their homes to pay their mortgages.

'There has also been a tremendous amount of change in legislation. We have had the Social Security Act of 1986, then the Housing Act of 1988, and now we have the Community Tax. This has put great pressure on our advisers, and they have had to learn a whole new lot of legislation, and our clients have found that life has become more complicated.'

The setting up and running of Citizens Advice Bureaux, costs money. Some of the expense is borne by the Department of Trade and Industry, who pay for the training of every CAB adviser, the national information system used and the professional support staff, (at the ratio of 2 paid staff for an average of 20 volunteer staff.)

The local authority pays for the actual running of the Bureau (rent, rates, fuel, telephone and postage, plus travel and expenses of volunteers.) It also pays for the salaries of the paid staff needed to guarantee the effective use of the free time given by the volunteers and the Bureau management committee.

At the end of the day, of course, it is the tax and rate payers who foot the bill, but who could possibly begrudge public money spent on something as worthwhile as the CAB? Without it, Saffron Walden would have a lot more problems on its hands!

—— • ——

The surprising thing about Church Street is, the number of beautiful houses to be found there, and not always immediately discernible to the unpractised eye. These houses were built by the wealthy and influential in the 18th and 19th centuries, and incorporate some of the best architectural features of their time.

Starlings (No.20 Church St) is just such a house. Step over its unpretentious threshold and you enter late Georgian elegance.

Nos. 16, 18, 20, 22 and 24 Church Street – 1989.

It was built by Thomas Welby in about 1753 and occupied by the Starling family from 1804 until the first decade of the 20th century.

The Starlings came to Saffron Walden from Scotland, possibly sometime in the 18th century. Rating lists for the 1790s record William Starling as living in a cottage at Commons End. (Common Hill?) Later, in 1804, he moved to No.20 Church Street from where he, and subsequent generations of Starlings, carried on a wine and spirit merchant's business.

William died in 1808, and his widow appears to have continued with the business with the help of other members of the family - John in 1812 and then James in 1824.

A great feature of No.20 however is, the wonderful cellars, dug out of the pure chalk and lined at a later date with brick. Whether these were there when the Starlings first moved in, or whether they were made subsequently, is not clear. There is no mention of them in the rating lists until 1839, but the present owner of No.20, Mr. Kenneth Reed, says that he believes that at least one of the cellar archways is extremely old.

By the mid-19th century, the Starlings were notable members of the community, and one of them, James, became Mayor of Saffron Walden in 1854.

But by the turn of the century, they had ceased to trade, and rating lists for 1911 show that No.20 belonged to Walter Emson (of Emson Tanner). By 1915 the house was empty, to be bought later by the baker, Mr. David Miller senior, who sold it almost immediately to Mr. Thomas Reed the Antique Dealer. (Down Your Street - Part One - pages 172-173).

When Thomas Reed died at the age of 90, his daughter Julia, and her husband Charlie Farnham moved into No.20 to look after her mother. (Down Your Street - Part One - pages 173-175). And when Mrs. Reed senior died in 1939, Julia, by common consent of the rest of the family inherited the property.

But after living there for a few years, the Farnhams, decided that, although No.20 was a splendid house, it was a little too large for them. Besides, both their daughters, Maisie and Janet were now married, and tragically their only son, David, had been killed whilst serving in the R.A.F. during the second World War.

By this time both George's sons had entered the family business, and Kenneth, on hearing that his cousin was going to sell her house realised this would present a problem because, a lot of surplus stock from No.20 Castle Street had always been stored at No.20 Church Street. So he decided to go to see Mr. Edmund Land, of Adams & Land, the Solicitors.

Mr. Land was somewhat taken aback when young

79

Kenneth Reed, a bachelor of 26, said he wanted to buy No.20 Church Street.

'Have you any money?' he asked. Kenneth replied that he had a little, so Mr. Land rang Mr. Jennings the Estate Agent of Cross Street to enquire how much was wanted for No.20, and without turning to consult Kenneth, told Mr. Jennings to 'put it down to me'.

'Well, congratulations young Reed,' he said as he put the 'phone down, 'you've just bought a house!'

'Thank you very much Mr. Land,' said Kenneth, 'but would you mind telling me how much I have paid for it?'

Even today, 43 years later, Kenneth Reed still smiles at the episode. 'I think I must be the only person in Saffron Walden to buy a 10 room town house and not know how much he paid for it!' (He actually paid £2,500).

Kenneth did not live in the house himself until 1957 when he married Joan Downham, daughter of Arthur and Evelyn Downham of Thaxted Road. Their romance had blossomed through their connection with the United Reformed Church in Abbey Lane. And Joan admits to being a very forward young hussy with a schoolgirl crush on her Sunday School teacher.

Over the years Joan and Kenneth have lovingly restored the old house to its former elegance, closing off the top storey and concentrating on the ground and first floors. And although they have no family, they really enjoy their home, and love to give parties - often for various charities - whenever they can. This is when their beautiful first floor Adam-style drawing room comes into its own - a room which took five years' holiday-money to renovate.

Kenneth, now 69, has, unfortunately had to retire from the family business, which is still carried on by his brother Clifford, and Clifford's son, Martin. He has also, sadly, had to retire from lay-preaching. 'Shades of my grandfather,' he says, 'but I'm afraid, unlike him, I never walked to the churches where I preached, Joan used to act as my chauffeur.'

Joan herself, is a driver for Uttlesford Community Transport, and it was her idea to start the bric-a-brac shop next door to the house, which has proved so popular over the years. So now, instead of buying a bottle of brandy or wine at the shop next door to No.20 Church Street (called Starlings in memory of the Starling family) local people who know, go there for that little, useful something-or-other, they can't find anywhere else.

———— • ————

Goddards' butcher's shop, No.19 Church Street, stands empty and waiting. Whatever happens next in the long history of this 15th century building, one thing is certain, it will never be a butcher's shop again.

Generations of Walden people have queued outside these premises, sometimes because of acute food shortages, and at other more affluent times because, the shop itself was rather small.

For over a hundred years meat has been sold on these premises, and, for probably just as long, livestock slaughtered at the rear.

According to old rating lists, William Barker appears to have been the first butcher to trade here between 1872 and 1901 or thereabouts. Later, in 1911, the name of Hubert Britton appears on the rating lists for No.19.

In 1933 Hubert Britton sold his business to Tom Goddard, a young man who had previously worked as his assistant. Tom had left his employment to volunteer for the army during the first World War. On his return, he went to work at the Cement Works in Thaxted Road, with the idea of earning enough money to buy his own butcher's shop.

By 1922 Tom had enough money to buy a pork butcher's shop at No.2 Bridge Street, and a year later married his sweetheart Edith Lacey. Edith was a local girl whom he met at the Fair in Swan Meadow one August Bank Holiday.

There was no slaughterhouse attached to the Bridge Street premises, so Tom used one behind the Queen's Head in Littlebury. For convenience sake, he bought a cottage nearby, but poor Edith was most unhappy at having to live in a house without running water and other mod cons.

But when he bought his Church Street shop, she was delighted, and it was here that her youngest child, her only

81

daughter, Sheila was born. They already had two sons, Richard and Norman, who were eventually to enter the family business alongside Tom's three brothers, George, Stanley and Reginald.

The business prospered, and soon the old horse drawn van which Tom had used for delivering meat was replaced by four motor vans delivering within a 20 mile radius of the town.

It would be impossible to talk about Goddards without mentioning their sausages. The sausage recipe was perfected by Tom himself and remained a closely guarded secret. So famous were Goddards' sausages that, at Christmas time, between two and a half to three tons of them were made to meet the demand.

Tom Goddard and his brothers Stanley and George, all died at comparatively early ages (Tom was only 52). Reginald, who retired in 1977, died in the early months of 1989. And when, in September 1988, this old-fashioned, old-established family business closed its doors for the last time, another chapter in Saffron Walden history ended.

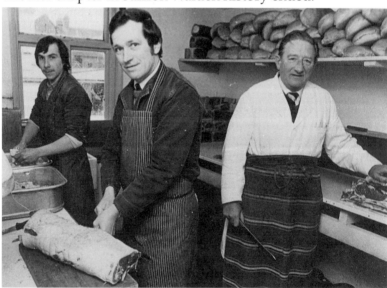

Mr. Richard Goddard (right) inside the family butcher's shop, Terry Start (centre) and Adrian Roberts (left).

Referring once again to old rating lists however, we find that these premises were once occupied by Henry Gatward, son of Thomas Gatward, the clockmaker.

The Gatwards were a very ancient clockmaking family who began their business in London in 1693. William Gatward and his son Thomas came from Hitchin to Walden in 1802, and lived at Freshwell House in Freshwell Street. Later, Thomas moved to George Street, and then about 1847 to Church Street. But previously, another member of the Gatward family had lived in Church Street - Roger Gatward - appearing in the rating lists in 1801, and disappearing from them in 1819.

Thomas died in 1863, and must have left Church Street in the early 1850s, or perhaps moved in with his son Henry, who lived at No.21 from 1836 until 1850, when the property passed into the hands of Martin Gatward (Henry's son?).

Where Henry moved to is not clear, but wherever he was he was certainly carrying on the family tradition, because in 1911 we find him living with his family in Cross Street in the shop which older generations will always associate with his son, William Arthur Gatward. (Down Your Street - Part Two - pages 162-165).

——— • ———

No.23 Church Street known as Cromwell House, is a 15th century house with a 17th century wing added at the rear extending southwards, and windows dating from 18th and 19th centuries.

But how many people remember No.23 when it was the home - perhaps the first home - of the Saffron Walden Weekly News? This would be about 1913 and probably the News occupied one room at the front of the building only, the rest of the premises being occupied by Mr. Burton the tailor.

Previously, from about 1840 until 1900, No.23 had been the home of another tailor, Mr. W. Redhead and his family.

But strictly speaking Cromwell House, was originally No.31 Church Street, part of what we now know as The Sun Inn complex, which also includes numbers 25 and 27. And -

so it is said - it is called Cromwell House because it was Cromwell's headquarters when his men entered the town. (But this has never really been proved.)

Although No.25 has not been a dwelling house for over 60 years, it was once the home of Mrs. Gladys Sutton. She was born here in 1917, the youngest of the five children of David and Ada Housden.

David Housden was a painter and decorator, one of the last painters and decorators in the town to mix all his own paints. This he did in a shed at the bottom of the Sun Inn yard, which would have been part of the old stables. He also used to help out at Whitehead & Days's, the monumental masons, when times were slack, and many an old tombstone in Walden bears his handiwork.

The Housden's cottage had three bedrooms, one of them, the room over the carriage-way with the pargetting depicting Tom Hickathrift and the giant. And like all the cottages in Walden at that time, mod cons were few. But at least they did have gas - downstairs - but upstairs it was a case of 'to bed with a candle' at night.

Growing up in Church Street in the early decades of this century, was a completely different way of life to the one experienced by children today. The noise of the pigs squealing as they were brought to the slaughterhouse of Mr. Britton the butcher (later Goddards) was as familiar to Gladys as was the ringing of the church bells which she missed so much when she moved away to marry her sweetheart, Percy Sutton from Gold Street. 'And I still do miss the bells,' she says.

Percy and Gladys, of course, will be remembered by all those who ever visited Walden Cinema at the top of the High Street. Percy was chief projectionist and Gladys cashier and usherette. After it was burned down in 1950, it was rebuilt and Percy and Gladys returned as manager and manageress until it finally closed in 1970 and demolished to make way for the block of flats now called The Maltings.

Someone else who grew up in Church Street almost at the same time, is 67 year-old Mrs. Peggy Selby, who came to No.27 Church Street with her parents, Arthur and Jennie Thake in 1923.

Percy and Gladys Sutton.

Those gentlemen who played football for the town during the inter-war period will remember Mr. Arthur Thake who used to drive Raynham's coaches, and had the responsibility of taking the local football team to their venues - and more importantly - getting them back home safely again.

Like Mrs. Sutton, Mrs. Selby grew up with the familiar sound of the church bells, and misses them very much because 'they don't ring like they used to!'

She remembers Church Street when, as children, they could play games in the middle of the road - 'children can't do that today.

Once I broke a window in the Miss Collins' house (Turner Collins' sisters) with my spinning top. It cost my father two shillings to replace it and that was a lot of money in those days.'

She also recalls Skingle House when it was a private house, and she and her brother (Arthur Robinson Thake now living in Newmarket) would go there to carol sing at Christmas, to be rewarded with halfpennies and farthings saved especially for the occasion. And she remembers Arnold's cafe right on the corner of the crossroads - now part of Lankester Antiques, and the Misses Harts who kept the woolshop (now another antique shop).

'There was also Scrimshaws, that was before Vincents came, they sold furniture and hardware. In fact,' she pats the sofa we are sitting on, 'this sofa came from Scrimshaws.'

When Peggy Thake married in 1943, she and her husband Leonard, a builder by trade, continued to live at No.27, in order to look after her recently widowed father. And they have stayed on ever since, despite the fact that they both love Eastbourne and had planned to retire there.

But when the time came, they felt that there is no place quite like Saffron Walden, and they would miss their friends terribly if they ever moved away.

Walking through the waggon-way arch of the Sun Inn we come to the old stables and find David and Terry Tedman who trade under the name of Whitehead & Day, Monumental Masons.

The business is an 18 year-old father and son partnership starting when David persuaded his father, a representative for J. Day & Son, undertakers of Bishop's Stortford, to acquire the old-established monumental masons' business of Whitehead & Day on Common Hill.

David explained that the "J. Day" of Bishop's Stortford has nothing to do with the "Day" of Whitehead & Day, and that when they took over the business, the owner was Mr. Eric Ray who later moved to Newmarket. And added that the origins of the business are documented as far back as 1857, borne out by an entry in the Town Almanack for 1886 under "Stonemasons" giving the names "Whitehead, Osborne - Common Hill". Which means this must be one of Saffron Walden's oldest businesses.

David is a true craftsman. He served his apprenticeship in all the crafts associated with the memorial trade, including carving and masonry cutting, and finally majoring in letter-cutting.

'No it is not a morbid occupation,' was his reply to the obvious question.

'It is a very personal business to be in though. A monument is not the sort of thing which people shop around for. A bereaved person will go to someone they know when they are looking for a monument, and for this reason we have a very close connection with Peasgoods the local undertakers, who, for convenience sake, forward our catalogue on our behalf.'

During the 20 years he has been in the trade, David has noticed that there has been a move away from white marble monuments towards black and dark grey granite. He thought that this is because people are more affluent these days and can afford polished granite, which wears better than white marble. He also pointed out that there was quite a distinction between what is allowed in cemeteries and what is allowed in churchyards.

Cemeteries, it appears are more concerned with the size of the monument, rather than the material it is made of. Whereas a churchyard requires a monument in keeping with a country churchyard, which rules out polished black granite and white marble. Unpolished granite and stones such as York, Portland, blue or green slate and Nabrasina marble (an off white Italian marble) are all perfectly acceptable however. That is, providing the churchyard is "open". (Many churchyards, like our own parish churchyard, are now "closed". One exception in recent years to this rule was the late Lord Butler's grave, which has a green slate monument with classical Roman lettering - made by David.)

It seems that churchyard authorities carefully vet the inscriptions on the tombstones and come down heavily on verses they think are too flowery. But again, cemeteries are less particular.

Sometimes apparently, people's feelings tend to get the upper hand, and they request inscriptions which the Tedmans know they will regret later on. So they have to tactfully suggest that the client goes away and thinks about it for a while.

David's first job was cutting Hebrew hyroglyphics for a Jewish undertaker in London's East End, and he assured me that it takes ten years to become a really competent letter-cutter. There is also quite a skill in finishing off the letters, especially in the case of raised lettering, which requires the cutting to be infilled with lead, instead of the more usual gold or silver leaf which the Tedmans always use.

The Tedmans moved their business from Common Hill to the Sun Inn yard 15 years ago, when Mr. A.C. Cain, builder and undertaker, moved out. In those days the yard still retained many features of the old stables, including the enormous old cobblestones, which, for practical reasons have been replaced by cement.

Those old cobblestones, which sloped towards the centre of the yard for drainage purposes, must have been immensely difficult to walk upon, especially during wet or icy conditions but - what a pity they had to go!

Watching David working on a memorial stone prompted another obvious question - what happens if the letter-cutter gets a word wrong?

The answer came with great feeling, 'you're in real trouble!'

The Sun Inn complex 1910 shown here as "old houses".

Spending the odd half hour browsing amidst the past is a temptation few people can resist. And for this very reason there cannot be many people living in Walden or visiting Walden who have not entered the Old Sun Inn at sometime or other. Perhaps in the first instance out of curiosity, to see what the old building looks like from the inside, only to be captivated by the sheer expanse of books and wide variety of antiques to be found there.

It is probably the most striking-looking building in the town - the most featured in print, most photographed by tourists - most famous of all Saffron Walden's historic land marks.

It was here, that Cromwell and Fairfax stayed when Fairfax had his headquarters in the town during the Civil War.

And yet, the Old Sun Inn has had its inglorious moments, viewed by many at those times, perhaps, as a prime site for demolition and development standing as it does on the corner of Market Hill and Church Street.

However, it is thanks to a former Town Clerk, Mr. William

Adams, and his clerk, the late Mr. H.C. Stacey and Miss Mary Gibson, sole survivor of the Gibson family in the town, that this fine old building is still standing today. Mr. Adams, in the early 1930s, assisted by Mr. Stacey, set about appealing for local subscriptions to enable the property to be handed over to the National Trust. Miss Gibson gave generously to the fund.

Unfortunately, the early history of the Sun has been befogged by time and lost records. Experts have dated it from 14th and 15th centuries with later, 16th, 17th, probably 18th and 19th century alterations.

Certainly it never started its long life as an inn, but rather an early Hall House, converted into two houses at sometime later and later still an inn. Local records show that in 1789 the landlord was Joseph Parke, and the whole complex owned by "Mr. Gibson".

Following Mr. Parke there was a succession of landlords until 1870 when it is shown in old rating lists as "empty". After that date it would seem that it never again functioned as an inn, and appears to have been divided into five dwelling houses - Nos. 25 to 31 Church Street and 17 Market Hill. It remained like this for several decades, and is shown in old photographs with the caption "old houses in Church Street, Saffron Walden."

During all this time, the property remained in the hands of the Gibsons until it was handed over to the National Trust.

For several more years it still remained divided into separate dwellings. Eventually in the 1960s the lease was put up for sale and Mr. John Lankester and his wife Eileen bought the lease from the National Trust on a 300-year full-repairing basis.

Their intention was to open a shop specialising in antiquarian and topographical books. But later they found there was a demand for good literature and they finally settled for a full range of secondhand books combined with new books on art, antiques and allied subjects, plus antiques.

Now, 24 years later, their antiques and stock of 50,000 books (carefully classified and catalogued), covers the whole

W.R. Norman's butcher's shop (former Isaac Marking's) with manager, Herbert Warner (left).

of the ground floor of the building and includes No.17 Market Hill.

This property adjoins the Sun Inn, and many people will remember it as the Cromwell Cafe. The Lankesters acquired it 11 years ago and found, during alterations, that it must have been originally part of the Sun Inn complex, a fact borne out by the discovery of an original communicating doorway.

John, who at 77, considers himself semi-retired, still takes an active interest in the business, which is now run by Paul and his wife Marion. But on the occasions when things get really hectic, all the Lankester family lend a hand, including the two youngest members, Paul's sons, Nicholas (6) and Robert (5).

It was Paul who pointed out to me the various interesting features of the interior of the Sun, including the original doorway, now blocked-up, and the Solar which would have had a ladder leading to the sleeping quarters. He also showed me the hall of the original Hall House, panelled

91

with wood in the 18th century, where an extra floor had been put in. And told me that, in the roof-space above, soot belonging to the 17th century can still be found on the beams.

But the most distinctive feature of the Old Sun Inn is the wealth of pargetting which dates from the 17th century, and the most interesting being the figures of Tom Hickathrift and the Wisbech Giant.

(Tom Hickathrift, a young East Anglian carter of "incredible strength", reputed to lift a haystack on his fork, is said to have felled with Giant with his axletree, using his cartwheel as shield.)

The mysterious "leg" which also appears on the pargetting is believed to denote that, at one time, this part of the building was used as a Hosiery.

——— • ———

Now as we continue on our way along Church Street, we cross over the road and walk along the northern side of the street for a little while.

First of all we pass No.22, a large house converted into flats, which at one time belonged to the Starling family. But many of the older residents in the town will remember No.22 as the aptly named Flora Club, a social Club for the exclusive use of Mr. Gustave Engelmann' s male employees, which continued to operate from the 1920s until the 1950s.

Later, in the 1960s, No.22 became the venue for the Saffron Walden Over Sixties Club.

Now we come to the crossroads, where Church Street, Museum Street and Market Hill all meet. These crossroads are believed to be unique, in that they have remained unchanged throughout the history of the town. On each corner stands a historically interesting building, the Sun Inn, of course, being one of them.

But here, on the north-west corner - officially known as No.24 Church Street - we find Weavers, an exclusive china shop, opened in 1984.

Department of Environment records describe this building as "a 16th century timber-framed and plastered house, altered in the 18th century."

But for some, No.24 will always be "Isaac Marking's butcher's shop." (Down Your Street - Part One - pages 203-208).

Opposite Weavers on the other side of the road is No.26 Church Street, another fine old timbered building, described by Department of Environment notes as "a 17th century timber-framed and plastered house."

Many people will remember No.26 as the wool shop, run by Miss Hart for many years, later by Miss Joy Hagger who became Mrs. Leslie Bidwell. But how many people know that this too was once a butcher's shop (actually a pork butchers) owned by Henry Swan Hill in 1886? And that earlier still, and for many decades from about 1819 until roughly about 1876, it appears in the rating lists as a "bakehouse" belonging to James Parker?

In recent years however, antiques have been sold from these premises. And it is difficult to reconcile the attractive exterior and elegant interior of Bush Antiques with earlier uses.

———— • ————

'Church Street was completely different from what it is now,' says Mrs. Nancy Pallett, speaking of her childhood days.

'For instance, up by the old castle there was a gate leading into a meadow where Mr. Marking (junior) used to keep his cattle. They used to drive them down the street past our door to the slaughterhouse. There was a hole in the door of the slaughterhouse which we children used to peep through. It all sounds rather terrible now - and I suppose it was very naughty of us!

Our house was right opposite the back of the King's Arms, and we would look out of our windows and watch the fights which went on when people had had too much to drink. We had a lovely ringside view! I have even seen a husband hit his wife. But I think people had a different outlook on life in those days.'

Mrs. Pallett, the daughter of Mr. Harry Nash, chauffeur-mechanic for Raynhams Garage in the High Street, was born at No.32 Church Street in 1920.

Mrs. Daisy Nash (seated) with her sister Lily and daughters Nancy (left) Molly (centre) and baby Marjorie.

Her father, she says, was a great favourite with the elderly ladies in the town, who all preferred to book "Harry Nash" whenever they wanted a driver. When he died at the early age of 54 from wounds he received in the first World War, her mother, Mrs. Daisy Nash was left to bring up her family of eight children, three boys and five girls.

But people were, indeed, different in those days, and Mrs. Pallett remembers especially the kindness of Mr. Isaac Marking who always gave the family a big joint of meat every weekend.

94

Like most of her contemporaries, little Nancy Nash was educated first, at Museum Street School and then South Road. After leaving school, she tried one or two jobs before eventually settling down to work at Woolworths, where she stayed until she married her first husband.

She now lives in Rowntree Way with her second husband, Mr. Ron Pallett, who for many years before he retired, was a Post Office counter clerk at the Post Office in the High Street.

Mrs. Pallett has two sons, Jimmy MacIntosh, the son from her first marriage, wellknown by Jazz enthusiasts in the town, and Graham, the son of her second marriage.

Department of Environment notes describe Nos. 30 and 32 Church Street as all one "16th-17th century timber-framed and plastered house, altered in the 18th and 19th centuries". Numbers 34 and 36 are also all one timber-framed and plastered house, believed to be early 19th century, but probably incorporating an earlier building, according to the Department of Environment notes.

We must remember, that during the 18th and 19th centuries Walden, like many other parts of the country, experienced a population explosion, and a lot of the larger houses in the older parts of the town were made into tenements. And this obviously happened to a number of the houses in Church Street.

Adjacent to No.36 is Johnson's Yard, a delightful surprise in the heart of this busy part of town. Here, tiny 17th century cottages nudge elbows with their late 20th century counterparts.

Two of them, Nos. 2 and 3, shelter with their backs half-hidden beneath the Castle grounds while their minute gardens bask in the southern aspects of the town. These two, and No.1 are all that remains of the original Johnson's Yard and the Iron Foundry which gave it the name.

Johnson's Iron Foundry was established on this site in 1810 or thereabouts. Rating lists show an ironmonger's shop as well as a foundry which continued to be run as a family business, until 1920, when it was bought by Mr. C. Medcalf. When the business changed hands, the foundry ceased, and the yard, its buildings and cottages were bought by Mr. George Reed, the Castle Street Antique Dealer.

Mr. Clifford Reed, George's youngest son, told me that at that time his father was doing house removals as well as running his antique business, and his reason for buying the yard was because he wanted a suitable place to put the van as well as room for storage purposes.

'My father built a shed for the van on a piece of ground next door to No.1. Later - much later - we sold No.1 along with the shed, and a few years ago the shed was pulled down and an extension built to No.1 in its place.'

Gradually the foundry, with its large chimney and outbuildings, fell into disrepair, and eventually, Johnson's Yard - apart from cottages 2 and 3, were sold to a property developer, who converted the old buildings into attractive dwellings.

Retired schoolteacher, Mrs. Evelyn Downham, has lived at No.2 Johnson's Yard for the past 14 years. She was born in the nearby village of Newport 82 years ago, the youngest child and only daughter of Herbert Choppen, a member of the local agricultural engineering family of that name.

Herbert Choppen opened the very first garage in Newport, but left the village in 1912 to take up a post in Yorkshire. At the outbreak of the first World War he volunteered for the army, along with two of his sons.

Herbert and his eldest son - Wilfred - survived, but Cecil the second son died in a prisoner of war camp.

In 1921 his father (A.J. Choppen) asked him to take over the family business in the High Street (now Goddards Electrical shop), and the whole family moved back to Walden.

When Herbert left the family business to trade under the name of H.W. Choppen in Station Street, he moved his family from the house next door to the shop in the High Street to No.82 Thaxted Road. And it was here that Evelyn lived for the next 46 years of her life, staying on to look after her widowed father after her marriage to Arthur Downham.

Arthur, a plumbing and hot-water engineer, was, at the time of their marriage, working for the local Gas Company, but later, he also set up his own business. And many of the older generation in the town will remember him as Leading Fireman Downham of the Borough Fire Brigade.

Evelyn herself trained to be a teacher, and worked as a governess for two or three years before accepting a job at Henham Primary School. After a time she left Henham to teach at Debden Primary School. But like many teachers in the 1930s, she had to give up her job when she married, only to return again when the second World War broke out.

She looks back on those wartime days with wistful nostalgia.

'I have some very happy memories of the war. We used to have classes of 42 children, and a lot of them were lovely little evacuees from London. Everyone helped one another in those days, but after the war I don't think people cared so much.

I was a billeting officer and I also worked for the St. John Ambulance Brigade as part of my war work.'

Mrs. Downham continued teaching at South Road Infants' School (later R.A. Butler Infants') from 1939, until she retired in 1970. And even after her retirement she continued as a supply teacher for the next eight years.

Although she leads a very active life - walks a lot with her dog - 'I think a dog is a splendid thing for an elderly person' - enjoys country dancing, a favourite pursuit for the past 30 years - is a member of the Town's Women's Guild, a Friend of Radwinter Road Hospital, and is on the Hospital Trust Committee - she says she still misses her teaching.

Like many people of her generation, she has watched Walden change over the years, and whilst admitting we have to move with the times, she says she prefers the town as it was. She mourns the fact that it has become so urbanised, and thinks the idea of turning Swan Meadow into a car park is ludicrous. 'Apart from the Common it is the last green place we have.'

She also comments on the amount of rubbish lying around in the streets.

'There are so many complaints about dirty dogs, but responsible people walk their dogs out of the town. What about the people who throw cartons and other rubbish about the streets?'

Like most of the people I have spoken to during this long, slow walk up Church Street, her final words were in praise of the church bells - 'I love to hear the church bells. I can't understand people who buy a house near a church and then complain about the church bells ringing. As for the clock, I don't mind it striking, one gets used to it!'

——— • ———

Ten years ago Saffron Walden was almost unique in that it possessed more family businesses than almost any other town in the country. These businesses had individuality and gave a quality of service beyond the reach of any chain store or supermarket.

Scrimshaws decorated for the Coronation – 1953.

98

Unhappily, throughout the decade many of them closed their doors for the last time, leaving generations of customers to mourn their loss. Although Vincents, the ironmongers at Nos. 38 and 40 Church Street, could not claim to have attended to the needs of generations of customers personally, they were indeed, a family run business, carrying on a tradition established by Thomas Johnson in 1810.

In 1920 Thomas Johnson sold out to Mr. C. Medcalf who continued to trade into the 1930s when the business was bought by Mr. Leslie Scrimshaw. Mr. Derrick Kemp, who now lives in Bury, Lancashire, was born at Green Farm, Littlebury Green, recalls working for Mr. Scrimshaw in 1939 when he was 15 years old. He writes:-

"When I first went there the board over the shop still had Medcalf & Son on it.

Mr. Scrimshaw built it up into a well-established business long before Vincent's took it over. I got five shillings a week (25p) and I used to wear a khaki smock and serve behind a polished counter weighing out nails, screws, bolts, hooks etc. We sold lino, crockery, firewood, calor-gas, hardwood, plywood, pots, pans, and cut glass to size for the customers. You name it - Mr. Scrimshaw sold it - furniture, paint, wallpaper and keys cut by hand!

Business people from London would send their furniture to Mr. Scrimshaw for storage to get it away from the air-raids. Most of the furniture would be antique and was stored behind the shop in the original iron foundry."

Later, in perhaps the late 1950s or early 60s the business was sold yet again, this time to the Vincent family who, for the next 20 years, ran it on much the same lines as Mr. Scrimshaw.

Undoubtedly it was a unique experience to step over the threshold of this incredible shop. One felt as if all the clocks had stopped. There was a certain amount of muddle, but it was an orderly sort of muddle. You might not, quite not, know what exactly it was you were looking for, but you could describe it to the man in the khaki drill overall behind the wooden counter, and he would know just what it was you wanted.

But in the early 80s, after the death of Mr. Vincent senior, the shop ceased to trade. It was the end of an epoch, the irreplaceable had ceased to exist and was later converted into a private house.

Across the road from what was Vincents, is the rear of the Kings Arms adjacent to the site which was formerly part of Cleales Tractor Division. Earlier still in the 1930s and 40s, Mr. Badman the bootmaker had his premises on this site. He was a cobbler in the old tradition and used to hand-sew the soles of the shoes he repaired. During the war he was much in demand repairing boots and shoes for the Americans stationed at Debden and the British Army stationed in Audley End Park.

Entrance to the King's Arms –
1952.

This was also true of Mr. A.G. Coe's Blacksmith's shop. Mr. Coe probably carried on his business in what was once the barn and stables belonging to what is now No.33 Church Street, otherwise known as "The Grange."

Department of Environment notes describe The Grange as being "an early 19th century yellow gault brick house with a stuccoed front. Two storeys, with a three storey wing at the east end."

Dr. Roderick Lumsden who lives at The Grange told me that he believed that the two storey part of the house was probably built around 1835, but that rest of the house was very much older, and was actually a timber-framed building.

Early maps do show a large house on this site, with a curving garden wall, which would bear out Dr. Lumsden's theory.

Certainly The Grange is an extremely fine house, very large - 16 rooms in all - and at the time it was built, it would undoubtedly have had stables - only a rich man could afford to live in such opulence. Further, there is a gate in the garden wall, leading into what would have been the stable-yard at the time it was built.

Dr. Lumsden said the staircase leading from the entrance hall was added about twenty years after the 1835 extension, and appears to have been built out over the street, a curious feature of the house being, the actual paving stones on the floor of the entrance hall.

In 1851 Dr. Thomas Spurgin, a 53 year-old general practitioner lived here, with his wife Martha and their eight children, his assistant, a nurse and governess, plus four other servants.

Although Roderick Lumsden is not a medical doctor himself - he has a Ph.D. in Electronics - he told me that The Grange had always been a doctor's house.

His own father, Dr. Kenneth Lumsden F.R.C.S. bought the house and Practice from Dr. J. Dudgeon in 1934, and lived here with his wife, Margaret, and their two sons, Gavin and Roderick, until his death in December 1967. (Gavin married Stella Howson, daughter of local author Harry Howson of Debden Road, and now lives in Little Walden.)

101

Dr. Lumsden will be remembered by many people in the town, not only as a general practitioner but also as surgeon at the General Hospital in London Road.

If rating lists are correct, Dr. Dudgeon succeeded Dr. Atkinson in the Practice who in turn succeeded Dr. Harley, who probably succeeded Dr. Spurgin!

Number 44 Church Street is the home of Mr. Raph Silver and his wife Gill. Raph is Chairman of the Saffron Walden Society and former ardent fighter against the proposal to bury the last bit of rural Walden under tons of concrete to make a car park.

With regard to the latter, he says: 'obviously I am disappointed about the Swan Meadow Car Park scheme going ahead. I do not think the authorities have really thought out what will be the planning incentives as a result of Swan Meadow, and that is a big danger. In the last Local Plan the Council said development on the scale of the South and East side of the town must never happen again. But now I foresee that development on that scale could easily happen on the north-west side of the town unless we have a coherent planning policy.'

Five years ago Raph Silver and his wife Gill didn't know Saffron Walden existed. Both were born in Liverpool, met at Durham University, and moved South soon after their marriage when Raph, a newly qualified lawyer, got a job in Cambridge.

They had been living in Cambridge for ten months before they discovered Saffron Walden, and then it was only by accident. Driving to a wedding in Brentwood, a flat tyre made them pull off the road into Caton's Lane Car Park to change the wheel. It occurred to them that the town was worth a return visit, so on the way back from the wedding, they stopped to have a look around and decided there and then that it would be a nice place to live.

But property in Walden was almost as expensive as in Cambridge, and even a down-payment on a small cottage in London Road was out of the reach of a newly married couple. Then, an incredible thing happened. Raph won £1,000 on the Times Portfolio Competition, which enabled them place a deposit on the cottage.

They moved into their little house in London Road in May 1985, and settled down to what, at first, seemed a rather lonely life in Saffron Walden. Raph out at work in Cambridge all day, Gill working in management for the Health Service in London, it left no opportunity to make friends in the town.

Later Gill got a job with the Housing Association in Cambridge, dealing with people with special housing needs, but even so, she still found she wasn't making friends. So she decided she must do something about the situation by getting involved in local activities.

She joined CND (became a member of the Committee and served two years as Chairman) the Green Party and Amnesty International and was out so much in the evenings that Raph began to complain.

Then the issue of Swan Meadow surfaced and a public meeting was called. Gill suggested that Raph go and see what it was all about.

The meeting was packed, and he realised that it was obviously a very controversial argument.

'I remembered reading some stuff about planning permission and things, and the impression I got was, that those who were against it had a good argument and needed help in the presentation of their argument. Secondly, I felt that the Council were riding rough shod over people's wishes. So I put my name down as someone who could possibly help - and it snowballed from there!

The issue completely took over my life for the next 18 months before the Public Inquiry. In fact for the four months prior to the Inquiry it was Swan Meadow and nothing else!'

Now the battle has been fought and lost, he insists that he does not regret the time and effort he put into opposing the Car Park scheme, and that it has all been worthwhile.

'But there's one thing I am absolutely sure about - I have absolutely no intention of lying down in front of the bulldozers when they move in! I am a lawyer, and I view the Swan Meadow Car Park scheme exactly as if it was a case I had lost, even though I am absolutely certain my client is innocent.'

Shortly after the Public Inquiry into the Swan Meadow Car Park scheme, the Traffic Scheme started. And Raph says he thinks it was a combination of the Council having to justify their actions on two fronts, that led to a general feeling that there were a lot of people concerned about the town, who were not committed to the town but felt they could make a greater contribution if they banded together. It was the success of the Traffic Group which sparked off the formation of the Saffron Walden Society.

Although Raph felt he was "burnt out" after the Inquiry into Swan Meadow, and did not want to take any part in the formation of the Saffron Walden Society, someone certainly must have twisted his arm, with the result that he became Chairman.

Despite the fact that the Society is not yet one year old, it has already made an impact on the town.

'One thing we have achieved,' says Raph, 'is, that the Town Council is now interested in knowing our views on certain matters before they make representation to the District Council - so we are being listened to.

However, there are certain people who think we have a political bias. And that is not true. We are certainly not a left-wing organisation and we have a lot of conservative members - spelt with both big and little "Cs"!'

Like a lot of people who have chosen to live in Saffron Walden (or near it for that matter) they feel extremely hurt when some of the local people, born and bred, suggest they have no right to express their opinion as to what happens in the town.

'I am now in partnership in Cambridge - Thomson & Co., of Castle Street - we are a young firm, and my branch of the Law is Criminal Litigation, and for practical reasons it would be far better and cheaper for me to live in Cambridge. But we both love the town so much - whenever you go out you always meet someone you know - and living here gives life such a nice balance.'

But why did they move from their dear little cottage in London Road to No.44 Church Street? Gill laughs, 'it was so tiny! The rooms were so small we could barely move when we had visitors. And Church Street is so lovely, and so convenient, and although we don't have a garden - which is a pity - we do have an allotment where we grow our own vegetables.'

We now come to Nos. 46 and 48 Church Street which - surprisingly - do not appear in Department of Environment notes as listed buildings. And yet - a quick glance at the rear of the houses provides ample evidence of antiquity. Also, entries in rating lists indicate that these cottages were in existence in the early 18th century.

To the right of No.48 there is a small alleyway (blocked) which once lead to "Oxborrow's Yard", a group of cottages demolished in 1937.

Robert Oxborrow was a Shoe-maker whose premises were behind No.46 and 48 in 1886, and who owned one or two of the adjacent cottages. But "Oxborrow's Yard" must also have been "Black Swan Yard" in earlier times, because this name appears in Deeds for Numbers 46, 48 and 50 Church Street. Further, a note in the rating lists for 1843 indicates a Brewery somewhere near here. So it is quite possible that Johnson's Foundry was built on the site of an old Brewery.

Mr. Peter Rule, who has lived nearly all his life at No.48 Church Street, told me that it was almost impossible to dig in the garden without digging up old bricks. He said that the cottages - about six of them altogether - extended right back from the street. Which means that they must have adjoined Johnson's Yard.

Peter's parents, Jim and Sylvia Rule, bought No.48 in 1950, in the days when cattle still grazed in Castle Meadow, and what little traffic there was, could drive both ways down the street. Like a great many children in those days, young Peter - now 38 - spent a lot of his time playing games in the street, something that he and his wife Jean, dare not allow their own son, seven year-old Kevin, to do.

Peter went to St. Mary's School in nearby Castle Street and later to Newport Grammar School, then at the age of 17 he started work at Saffron Press. Now 21 years later, as a Buyer/Estimator for the Press, he finds that he must become a commuter when the company moves to new premises in the Docklands area of London.

When asked if he thought the town had changed much

105

over the years, Peter replied that it certainly had - and not necessarily for the better. But he categorically came out in favour of the Swan Meadow Car Park scheme, saying - that living in Church Street and not having anywhere to park his own car safely - it "bugged" him to think that people were against something which the town needed badly.

'I appreciate that Swan Meadow is a bit of a beauty spot to some people, but I think it is as good a place as any for the car park considering all the other possibilities.'

Educational Psychologist Dr. Margaret Peters, who lives at No.50 Church Street (Castle Lodge) on the other hand, is extremely distressed at the prospect of turning Swan Meadow into a car park. Like so many people who, although not born in Walden, enjoy living in such historically interesting and delightful surroundings, she feels apprehensive at the last piece of rural Walden being turned into a car park.

The Peters family came to Thaxted in 1948, lived for a time in Bridge Street, then moved to Castle Lodge nine years ago.

Although Castle Lodge, standing as it does on Bury Hill, gives the impression of a large residence, it is, in fact, quite a modest house.

Dr. Peters told me that the Deeds go back to 1582, in the 24th year of the reign of Elizabeth I, in a transaction between Lord Thomas Howard and Lady Katheryne Howard (his wife) of Audley End of the one part, and Roye Bibbye of the other part. Bibbye was a Chamberlain (the equivalent of Alderman) in 1579 and Treasurer (equivalent of Mayor) in 1582.

The original house was a small timber-framed house with a 70ft well outside, (now incorporated in the house and filled in). In 1819 it was clad with brick and extended with staircase and panelling. Later, in 1878, the bay windows and porch were added. This latter alteration is confirmed by a note written in pencil on the porch "Charles Hardwick. Burried (sic) today, July 9th 1878." And another note in another place "This porch was made June 18 1878".

Records show that the fortunes of Castle Lodge, like many old houses in Saffron Walden, have waxed and waned. Built in the first instance for an important man, in 1822 until 1824 it was occupied by paupers. Previously, in 1801, it was the home of Susanna Day, the Quaker lady whose journal "A Memoranda for the Help of Recollections" (1787 to 1804) is still retained in the Friends' House in the High Street.

In her journal, Susanna Day writes of hearing the sounds of the Fair on the Common and watching a cowhouse on fire in Castle Street.

The Days (Thomas and Susanna) lived in Castle Lodge from 1801 to about 1805, although it appears as if Thomas died somewhere between 1803 and 1804, because later entries refer to "Mrs. Day" only.

Dr. Peters says that she remembers her first night spent in Castle Lodge. It unhappily co-incided with the last night of the Circus on the Common and she can still recall the screams of the animals in the trucks as they moved away.

She feels very strongly about travelling circuses, and a short while ago when the Circus was visiting Saffron Walden Common she got up a petition, which 500 people signed. Unfortunately the authorities concerned with such matters dismissed the petition on the grounds that the Circus 'brought money into the town.'

In addition to her love of animals, Dr. Peters says she 'busies herself with the inter-Church world wide concern known as Justice, Peace and the Integrity of Creation,' an ecumenical movement which is preparing for a World Conference to be held in Seoul this coming Spring. She is also Clerk of the Friends' Meeting, a position she has held since January 1985.

But many people will remember Castle Lodge when it was the home of Mr. C.S.D. Wade, Clerk to the Peace, and senior partner in the firm of Wade & Lyall, the local solicitors in Hill Street.

Number 37 Church Street has been the home of Saffron Brokers for the past 20 years. And it was here that I met 46 year-old Keith Wardley, Managing Director of Saffron Brokers. Strictly speaking, Mr. Wardley cannot actually claim to be a local man - he was brought up in Littlebury. He was however, born in Saffron Walden - actually brought into the world by Dr. Justinian Bartlett, at the General Hospital in London Road.

Because at that time his father was working at Engelmann's Nursery, he went to The Boys' British School, and was taught - he says proudly - by Mr. J.P. Elsden 'as was my father before me.'

But, by the time he was ready to leave The Boys' British, his parents had moved to Duxford. So, despite the fact that he had been destined for The Friends' School, having won a scholarship, he actually attended the Cambridge County High School for Boys.

After leaving school he went straight into an Insurance Office in Cambridge. Then, five years later came back to Saffron Walden to join S.A.I.S. Ltd. (Secretarial and Insurance Services) in Museum Street.

'This was in 1965,' says Mr. Wardley, 'and by that time the secretarial services side of the business had diminished. The firm had become a limited company, and needed a manager to look after the insurance side of the things. And in those days my office was what is now the gents toilet at the Conservative Club!

I really enjoyed coming back to Saffron Walden. Most of the boys who were my contemporaries at the Boys' British were now business men in the town, and it was nice to belong to a small, friendly community where everyone knew everyone by name.'

Five years later Keith Wardley was made a partner in the company which he now owns, and in 1969 Saffron Brokers moved to their present premises - an early 19th century house - in Church Street.

With the advent of the Financial Services Act three years' ago, the company took the opportunity to form Saffron Brokers Life and Pensions Co. Ltd., specialising in life insurance and pensions. That was when Mr. Bruce Davidson, co-director of this branch of the business, joined the firm.

Speaking of the future, Mr. Wardley said that with the prospect of the growth of Stansted Airport it was possible that the town would double in size, and that would inevitably bring more business. But personally he was happy with the town the size it is now, and he enjoyed being a small-town business man in a small town.

Janet Riley Fabrics

* **Curtain Fabrics**
* **Dress Fabrics**
* **Haberdashery**

5 Market Walk
Saffron Walden
Essex CB10 1JZ

Tel: 01799 527694

CHAPTER THREE

Common Hill

First published in the Saffron Walden Weekly News
March 8 – April 19, 1990

The Common was known in earlier times as "Castle Green", for obvious reasons. And from the Royal Tournament in 1252, when a Norman knight, Ernulph de Monteney was killed, right through numerous fairs, feasts and celebrations down to its present use - in part at least - as a Car Park - the Common has always played its part in the changing history of Saffron Walden.

Perhaps the most famous of all feasts held on the Common was the one held in 1814 to celebrate the defeat of Napoleon and his exile to the Isle of Elba. Certain public spirited gentlemen in the town decided to celebrate the occasion by providing a dinner on the Common for "the poor of Saffron Walden".

The 6th July was chosen as a suitable day, and 2,400 people (including various officials) sat down at 40 tables placed in a curved line forming an oval on the Common. The whole area was roped off with an orchestra at one end.

The amount of food purchased for the occasion was mind-boggling - 2,566 lbs of beef (3 oxes), 170 lbs of mutton, 274 lbs of suet, 11 bushels of flour, 442 lbs of plums, 1,548 eggs at 1d. each, 6 pecks of salt, 2,6088 penny rolls, 957 gallons of beer and $11^1/4$ lbs of tobacco.

All the cooking was done by volunteers, over 200 people who could not attend, were served with food in their own homes.

After dinner, everyone full of good cheer and 'high in expectation' gathered round to play games and enter various competitions.

The Common at the turn of the century.

Splendid though this celebration must have been, it was unfortunately a little premature because as we know, Napoleon escaped from Elba and landed in France on 1st March 1815!

But apart from celebrations, fêtes and fairs, the Common had other, more utilitarian uses. Certainly the housewives who lived in the courts and yards of nearby Castle Street, would have been lost without the Common for drying their clothes.

A century and more ago, every fine day would see rows of washing hanging between the trees at the top end of the Common close to Ashdon Road. It was not a practice approved of by all however. In 1863, at the General Quarter Sessions, the Grand Jury presented 'the drying of clothes at the top of the Common a dangerous and public nuisance'.

And again, three years later, the authorities stated that clothes overhanging the footpath at the top of the Common proved an inconvenience to the public traffic. (This, I suppose was quite reasonable as all the traffic would be horse-drawn, and a sheet or garment flapping in the wind could easily upset a nervous horse.)

112

Nevertheless, the practise of drying clothes on the Common appears to have been encouraged rather than discouraged, and posts were provided to support the washing lines on the "inner row of trees" - previously hooks had been driven into the "outer row of trees". The Ordnance Map of 1877 clearly shows the position of these posts.

This practice of hanging-out washing on the Common continued up to just before the second World War, ending when the slum clearance scheme of the late 1930s demolished most of the property around the Castle Street area.

Many people will remember the auctions which were held from time to time on the Common, and a few - perhaps - the Horse Fairs. Others will remember the cricket pavilion, built in 1871, and removed to the Anglo-American Memorial Playing Fields in the 1954. For some, the memory of tobogganing when the Common was covered in snow, will recall vivid scenes of their childhood, and schooldays spent at the Boys' British.

In more recent years the Common has featured largely in acrimonious correspondence in the letters column of the

Pupils of the Boys' British on the Common, dressed for a school play – 1949. Convent in the background (demolished in the 1970s - now De Bohun Court).

Weekly News and there are many who believe a car park under the Common preferable to one in Swan Meadow.

But how many people realise that we were in grave danger of losing the Common altogether when it was threatened by enclosure in 1814? Fortunately thanks to the efforts of Atkinson Francis Gibson it was saved for all times.

The drinking fountain on the northern side of the Common was erected to celebrate Queen Victoria's Golden Jubilee. And the double row of young trees close by - Norway Maple, Turkey Oak, London Plane and others, were donated by various groups, organisations and individuals in the town to replace elm trees which fell victim to Dutch Elm disease a few years ago.

——— • ———

Common Hill on the western side of the Common came into being sometime around 1831 when a bridge was built over the Slade at Cates Corner. This meant that a road could be made for pedestrians and vehicles joining Hill Street with Church Street, Castle Hill and Ashdon Road.

But long before the road was made, No.10 Common Hill - Cromwell Lodge - had been built, or converted from buildings already standing there, by an obviously wealthy man who could afford horses, carriages and servants.

This elegant, three storey brick-faced house, is described by Department of Environment records as "an early 19th century red brick front probably to an 18th century house, with a return front to No.39 Church Street".

The present owners, Paul and Marion Lankester have spent ten years painstakingly and lovingly restoring this charming old building, with the result that it is now a delightful family home. Everything has been done with a sympathetic regard to the age and style of the property.

This is not surprising because as proprietors of Lankester Antiques & Books, at the Old Sun Inn, Church Street Paul and Marion naturally have a strong respect for the past.

Paul came to live at Cromwell Lodge when his family moved to Saffron Walden in 1964. When his parents

114

decided to move to Thaxted, Paul, very wisely bought the house from them. That was in 1975, and four years later, he married Marion, whom he had met in the shop.

It happened that Marion's brother had been helping out at Lankester Antiques during his college vacation, and Marion, who lived with her parents in nearby De Bohun Court, popped into the shop from time to time.

Like Paul, Marion's parents are not, strictly speaking, local people. Her father served in the R.A.F. and the whole family travelled around extensively. Finally they settled in Bishop's Stortford, but decided they liked Saffron Walden better.

In between restoring Cromwell Lodge, running the family business, bringing up their two sons, Nicholas (7) and Robert (5) Paul and Marion lead an extremely crowded life. Like all the Lankester family they are, of course, musical. Both are members of the Saffron Walden Choral Society, acting as Librarians - 'which means we store all the music'.

They are also keen conservationists and great believers in recycling. Marion, who is also a strong supporter of Greenpeace, said that they were extremely disappointed to learn that the District Council no longer want waste paper because of the lack of processing plants. She feels they have taken an enormous step backwards, and looks forward to the time when the Council provides aluminium and steel can banks, and a paper bank, alongside the bottle bank on the Common.

Quite a number of people will remember Cromwell Lodge when the Miss Vines lived there.

The last Miss Vine died in 1958 and a distant cousin inherited the property. The cousin, remembered childhood visits to Cromwell Lodge, when 'the wind from the Urals blew across the Common'. This fact, coupled with the great age of the property, made him think that the house would collapse one day. So he promptly sold his inheritance to a local farmer for £2,000, who paid cash on the spot - counting out the banknotes from his wallet! It was this farmer who later sold the property to Paul Lankester's parents.

'It was nice living on the Common. You saw everything that was going on,' says 85 year-old George Halls, who remembers Common Hill as it was over 40 years ago.

'During the war there was a big emergency water tank - 456 gallons it held. It's still there now, but they have filled it in.' He is speaking about the second World War of course, and the huge tanks of water to be found in public places in case of an incendiary bomb attack.

George Halls was born at Butlers Farm near Ashdon in 1905, and brought up by a foster-mother in Thaxted. When he left school he worked as a poultry plucker for a Thaxted

Jean (centre) and Janet (left) Halls and friend celebrating Janet's birthday on the Common.

farmer named William Coe. Later he left Mr. Coe to work first, on the building of the Thaxted Sewage works, and then at Gough's Maltings in West Road in Walden.

He lodged in Castle Street, with the friend - Jack Woodley - responsible for getting him the job at the maltings.

Jack Woodley drove a horse-drawn van for Robsons of Station Street. And often when he was going from village to village delivering goods - paraffin, cleaning materials, pots and pans and the like - he was accompanied by his young sister, Dora.

Dora was only 14 when George first saw her, but it didn't take him long to decide that she was the girl for him. 'But,' he says, 'it took me the next ten years to land her!' It seems young Dora had a boyfriend in London. But mother knew best, and hinted more than once that Dora would be better off with George.

The early decades of this century saw the decline of the malting industry in Saffron Walden, and after a few years George and Dora moved to Royston and George returned to poultry plucking. It was in Royston that their first daughter, Jean, was born. Then came the war, and the farm where George worked was sold, and so they returned to Walden, to live at No.7 Common Hill.

This was a tied cottage belonging to Engelmann's Nurseries where George now worked as a maintenance man. It was a job which suited him down to the ground because he confesses to never being happier than when he has a hammer in his hand.

(It was George who converted the Flora Club in Church Street into a club for the Walden Over Sixties.)

George stayed at Engelmann's until he retired in 1970, when he and Dora moved from Common Hill to No.18 Parkside. Sadly Dora died seven years later. But luckily both his daughters live quite near. (Janet his second daughter was born at No.7 Common Hill in 1951).

Both sisters, speak of Common Hill with great affection, remembering the happy times they had playing on the Common, and gathering wood for the bonfires for Guy Fawkes night. 'We used to store it in the cellar and dad used to go mad!'

Like their father they can recall some of the old folk who lived in the houses nearby, like one of the Miss Vines from Cromwell Lodge, who was a very tiny lady. And Miss Maudie Searle who lived at No.5 and whose father was Fred Searle, the coachman at the Rose & Crown.

They also remember the garden where Emson Close is now, and scrumping for the apples which grew there.

Now both are married with homes of their own but work

together in Janet's drapery and haberdashery shop in Market Row - Janet Riley Fabrics. (Down Your Street - Part Two - pages 179-180).

For many years now No.7 Common Hill, has been a private residence, and for seven of these, the home of Mr. and Mrs. Paul Tongue.

We now come to No.4 Common Hill, an attractive house set back from the road with a front garden alive with shrubs and flowers where once tombstones stood.

For well over a hundred years, Whitehead & Day (formerly Whitehead, Osborne) carried on their business as Monumental Masons at No.4 Common Hill. Although the business changed hands more than once throughout its long history, the name Whitehead & Day always remained. Even today the name is still perpetuated by Mr. Terry Tedman and his son, David, after they bought the business 18 years ago from Mr. E. Ray. Later the Tedmans moved to the Old Sun Inn complex and No.4 Common Hill was put on the market. (See Church Street pages 86-88).

Now No.4 is the home of Mrs. Joy Williams, widow of the author, Raymond Williams, whose books, both fiction and non-fiction, are published extensively both sides of the Atlantic.

Raymond Williams died suddenly two years ago at the age of 66, since when Mrs. Williams has engaged on the mammoth task of cataloguing his works and helping in the posthumous publication of two of his novels.

The first of these novels - People of the Black Mountains - was published by Chatto & Windus last year. A collection of short stories woven together in novel form, set in the borderland between England and Wales where Raymond Williams was born, it covers a time-span starting at the Ice Age, 23,000 B.C. and ending at 51 A.D.

The second part, continuing the theme, covers the period 51 A.D. up to 1400, will be on sale in August this year.

Mrs. Williams told me that her husband was particularly fond of this region and its people. And it was when they found a derelict cottage in the Black Mountains, which they bought and restored over a two year period, that he felt inspired to write what he intended to be a series of novels covering the history of the area.

Raymond Williams, a Fellow of Jesus College, Cambridge, was born in the village of Pandy in 1921. During the second World War he served in the 21st Anti-Tank Regiment, Guards Armoured Division, rising to the rank of Captain. Later, from 1974 until 1983 he was Professor of Drama at Cambridge.

He was a prolific writer with 30 books to his credit, six of them novels. He also contributed chapters to other publications, wrote over 200 literary reviews for the Guardian plus Television reviews for the Listener during the 1970s.

Mrs. Williams describes her husband as a cultural theorist, and says he was theoretically politically very active with a bias towards the left. They both belonged to C.N.D. (she still does) their membership starting from the days of the Aldermaston marches.

Joy Williams, herself was born in North Devon, and is a graduate of the London School of Economics. She met her husband during the war when the L.S.E. was evacuated to Cambridge. After their marriage in 1942, she became his research assistant, devoting her life to his work and bringing up their three children - two sons Ederyn and Madawc (both scientists) and one daughter Merryn Hemp, better known as Merryn Williams the writer on Victorian Novelists.

After Professor Williams retired in 1983 they realised that they were no longer tied to the "five mile limit" required of University Dons, and it was he who suggested that Saffron Walden would be a very pleasant place to live. It was just about the time that Caravans International (who bought the house from Whitehead & Day) went into liquidation, and No.4 Common Hill, which had been used as their "hospitality suite" came onto the market.

The works of Raymond Williams will be greatly missed in the realms of contemporary literature, and perhaps because of this, Jesus College is proposing to endow a Fellowship in his name in the near future. Also the Arts Council, of which he was a member, are intending to initiate the Raymond Williams' Prize. This is an award, to be divided between a small Publisher and the author, for a work of literary merit, exemplifying the general attitude towards ordinary people and their lives, 'because,' says Mrs. Williams, 'that is what his own work always embodied.'

Common Hill – 1990.

Much has been said and written about The Priory on Common Hill, but one fact has never been made clear, and that is, whether it ever was actually a Priory.

Certainly it is probably the oldest building this side of the Common. Department of Environment records describe it as "a 16th century timber-framed and plastered house, later divided into two houses" (Nos. 2 and 3). "The southern half, being the only original part remaining, was built in 1580, and the northern half added in the late 17th century. Both buildings altered in the 18th and later centuries, with the whole front faced in 18th century red brick."

John Player, writes of The Priory in his "Sketches of Walden" (1844), and says 'it is the belief that it was the residence occasionally of Sir Thomas Smyth' (See Market Place pages 11-12). John Player, continues by saying, 'it is now occupied as a ladies' school'.

It is not certain when the school was first opened. The 1851 Census shows "Ann Saunders - School Mistress" at this address, but old rating lists refer only to "house, stables etc."

By the end of the 19th century however, The Priory, was advertised as a school "Established for Young Ladies, conducted by Miss Erswell, assisted by an efficient resident governess." Whether the Miss Erswell in question was Miss Rebecca or Miss Elizabeth the advertisement does not say. Rating lists indicate Rebecca Erswell lived at the Priory from 1869 until about 1884 when the property appears to pass to Elizabeth Erswell who lived there until about 1915.

By 1920 the school had changed hands. Local historian, Mr. Cliff Stacey, in the journal of the Saffron Walden Antiquarian Society writes:-

"Between the wars Miss M. Cunningham had a private Junior School at The Priory (No.3). Later, perhaps sometime in the 1930s, Miss Cunningham moved her school to No.19 Audley Road where she continued to call it The Priory School."

The Priory – 1949.

Another wellknown name associated with The Priory is that of Mr. Cliff Welch the Veterinary Surgeon who had his practice at No.2 for many years. Described by many as 'a real country vet', in actual fact he had no formal training and never qualified. All his considerable skills were learned from his father, Mr. Percy Welch who moved his practice from Market Row (now Goulds) to Common Hill sometime before the first World War.

No.2 Common Hill appears to have been associated with a Veterinary Practice for over a hundred years. In the 1851 Census List we find an entry for "James Rule, Vet, age 55" at this address. A later entry in the 1886 Almanac refers to a "veterinary forge" under heading "Common".

Since 1974 however, The Priory has been restored to make one complete house again by the present owners, Mr. and Mrs. Russell Hawkes.

The Hawkes came to live at No.2 Common Hill in 1973, their next door neighbour at No.3 being Miss Elizabeth Day.

Miss Day died a year later, and although they only knew her for that one year, the Hawkes speak of their neighbour with great affection, describing her as a wonderful old lady, one of Saffron Walden's best known characters.

She was secretary at the General Hospital in London Road during the second World War, and also played in a local String Quartet. Many people will remember her as captain of the Golf Club, and others will remember the beautiful needlework she did. She was a member of the Royal School of Needlework and embroidered practically everything, and obviously inherited her talent from her mother who was an extremely skilled needlewoman.

Elizabeth Day lived at No.3 for fifty years, and when she died the Hawkes bought the house to add to theirs. Many of her possessions were put up for auction, and Tessa Hawkes bought one or two pieces, which she put back in the places where they had always been during Miss Day's lifetime.

During the 17 years they have lived at The Priory, the Hawkes have lovingly restored many of its original features, and take great delight in gleaning and treasuring any historical bit of information connected with the house which comes their way.

Because of this the Priory now has "Shakespeare's bedroom" (a room in what they call 'Miss Day's part of the house.')

Russell Hawkes feels there is some substance in the story that Shakespeare once slept at The Priory in 1610, when, as Director of the Company of the King's Players he was brought from London to entertain King James who was visiting Audley End at that time.

Shakespeare's friend - Master Holgate - owned The Priory, and to please his friends, Shakespeare obtained permission to perform one or two of his plays in the yard of the Rose & Crown (now Boots car park).

'If Shakespeare performed his plays in the yard of the Rose & Crown, which is so near here, then surely he would have slept at The Priory which, after all, was his friend's house?', argues Mr. Hawkes.

When asked what brought them to the town, the Hawkes laughingly admit that they came to Walden to get as far away from London as possible yet still be able to get up to town whenever they wanted. Which, means frequently for Tessa because, as a freelance specialist in Decorative Finishes - stencilling, ragging and marbling on furniture, ornaments and walls etc. – she finds herself with quite a few commissions in London as well as many other parts of the country.

Russell Hawkes, a partner in the firm of chartered accountants - Spicer & Oppenheim - retired from the City three years ago and now also works in a freelance capacity as a financial consultant.

They have four children, three girls and a boy, who all attended nearby St. Mary's School in Castle Street. Now the eldest, 23 year-old Polly is working as a 'maid of all work' in the British Virgin Isles, whilst her sister Lucia is in her final year at Durham University, reading Ancient History and Greek. Nineteen year-old Aidan is also at Durham University reading Social Anthropology, and Daisy the youngest member of the family is busy doing her A-levels at the Leys school in Cambridge.

Referring once more to John Player's "Sketches", wherein he draws attention to 'one of the piers of the old garden gate (of The Priory) yet in existence, and now forms part of a summer-house nearby.' This appears in Department of Environment notes as "part of a castellated red brick fronted gateway, now blocked, the front has the remains of moulded and panelled brick pilasters and a 3 light leaded window on the first storey. The north side is flint faced with red brick dressings and has a small battened door with a Tudor arch and a small window above with a Tudor arch."

This is an interesting little building, and unfortunately does not now belong to the Priory, but is at the moment used as a studio.

The car park belonging to Boots Chemists brings us to the end of Common Hill. Twenty years ago I could have written about the Rose & Crown, and the Brewery Tap which stood this side of the old hostelry. But no trace remains of the old Brewery Tap where the farm-workers drank whilst their masters refreshed themselves in the Rose & Crown. The Tap was burned to the ground during the fire which destroyed the Rose & Crown on 26th December 1969.

The Rose & Crown yard, now Boots' car park.

CHAPTER FOUR

Emson Close

First published in the Saffron Walden Weekly News
May 3 – May 31, 1990

Emson Close is once again the subject of controversy. Perhaps "once again" is the wrong expression to use in this particular instance because, the first time it was the centre of a conflagration was when Emson Close as such, did not exist.

What did exist, was one of the last remaining maltings in the town, which a few gallant and far-sighted people -

Demolition of the old Town Maltings.

including the late Dr. Kenneth Lumsden and his wife - fought to save. Unfortunately they lost their battle and the maltings were demolished almost overnight to make way for a new development of retail shops called "Emson Close".

Now, planning permission has been sought to turn a small car park, used by the business people working in Emson Close, into a block of offices. Thus demolishing an essential amenity as well as destroying the privacy of some of the residents on Common Hill.

What this part of the town looked like almost a hundred years ago can be seen from the map below. The map also shows buildings on the north-east corner of the Market Place which have since been demolished.

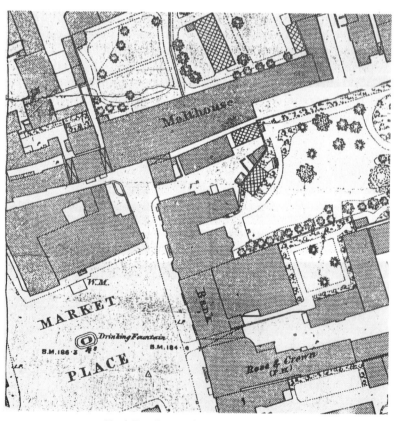

North East Corner of Market Place – 1894.

No. 10 Emson Close, once an old farmhouse.

Only one of these buildings remains standing now, No.10 Emson Close, a splendid 16th century timber-framed house with a 17th century addition fronting the Market Place. This is believed by some to have been the birthplace of Sir Thomas Smyth (or Smith) 1514-1577 (See Common Hill, page 120). This could well be true because it is said that he was the son of a sheep farmer, and this particular building was, indeed, once a small farm.

Unfortunately rating lists do not exist earlier than the late 18th century, and the first farmer recorded is a Mr. Mapletoft, with a later entry for 1790 giving the name of Joseph Martin "messuage, farm, land and lime kiln."

The choice of name for this development perhaps sprang from the proximity of the building now housing Eaden Lilley and Gayhomes, which was occupied by John Emson, miller, in the early 18th century. (See Market Place, pages 14-21).

No.10 Emson Close is now the office of Simon J. Lander & Co. Ltd., Insurance Consultants. Twenty-five year-old Simon is in partnership with his father Raymond Lander, and the company has occupied their present premises for the last two years. Originally they were at No.82 High Street.

Simon is occasionally helped out by his wife Theresa, who comes from Chelmsford. Both have a deep respect for the past and love the idea of working in one of the oldest, and historically interesting buildings in the town.

We now cross the road to No.9 Emson Close to visit the Evan Steadman Communications Group which was founded by local businessman Evan Steadman in 1972 as an advertising and public relations agency serving clients in the high tech world of electronics.

In July 1988 the Group was purchased by Robert Maxwell's Maxwell Communications Corporation, thus enabling Evan Steadman to devote more time to his great love - the world of theatre.

Continuing along Emson Close but walking back towards Market Hill we pass three more examples of late 20th century living. First the Launderet, modern equivalent of the old communal wash-houses, next Coral Bookmakers and thirdly, the Job Shop - an employment source unheard of before the second World War.

Emson Close – 1990.

130

Next we come to Kevin Henry Estate Agents, a young firm in every sense of the word, and another example of changing Walden. Twenty years ago, there were only three estate agents in the town, now estate agents appear almost round every corner. But although Kevin Henry Estate Agents have only been established since October 1988, their roots are firmly planted in the past.

Thirty year-old Kevin Moll (the Kevin part of Kevin Henry) came to Saffron Walden at a very early age and attended St. Mary's School in Castle Street. He is related to a well-known local farming family, and took his diploma in Rural Estate Management at The Royal Agricultural College at Cirencester. Later he became Branch Manager for the old-established firm of Edwin Watson Estate Agents in Saffron Walden.

Henry Rowe, 34, son of Mr. "Ted" Rowe, Senior Partner of Edwin Watson & Son in Saffron Walden, was born at Clavering and started his education at Dame Bradbury's School in Ashdon Road. For a time he worked as an estate agent in Australia before returning to his native Essex, where he became a Branch Manager for Edwin Watson in Bishop's Stortford before setting up in partnership with Kevin Moll.

Studio 2000 at No.3 Emson Close is a bright, modern, friendly hairdressing salon run by a highly successful husband and wife team, Patrick and Audrey Ray.

Patrick, an aeronautical engineer, decided there was no future in aeronautical engineering, and so became a hairdresser when he married a hairdresser - Audrey. That was 30 years ago. Now they own no less than three hairdressing salons!

Another old-established family firm is the Saffron Walden Laundry at No.2 Emson Close, one of the few family businesses left in the town.

Saffron Walden Laundry can trace its long history back to before 1897 when it was purchased from Mr. Arthur Titchmarsh by Mr. Gerald Southall whose descendants, the Southalls and the Griffiths run it today on the site of the original premises in Gold Street.

Mr. Stephen Griffith told me that the decision to open a

branch shop in Emson Close in the 1960s was a natural expansion of their business. Space allocated to receiving laundry and dry-cleaning had become rather limited in Gold Street, and with the nearby Common and Market Place for parking, the Company thought that Emson Close was an ideal site. The wisdom of this decision has more than proved itself over the last 25 years.

Mrs. Valerie Jacobs (née Braybrooke), has worked in the Laundry shop in Emson Close for 17 years. She is a real local - her grandparents used to keep the Red Lion in Castle Street - she herself was born at No.53 Castle Street, and she still lives in Castle Street - at No.37.

Valerie went into the offices of Emson Tanner as a clerk, as soon as she left school. (See Market Place, pages 18-21). She recalls Emson Tanner's as being 'a lovely, very friendly place, filled with the evocative smells of old-fashioned grocers' shops - dried fruit, cheeses and bacon curing.'

As befits a local girl she married a local boy, David Jacobs from Farmadine Grove, and later left Emson Tanner's to have her son Stephen - now an accountant. She returned in the early 60s just before the business was sold and the site redeveloped.

But although her memories of working at Emson Tanner's are remembered with affection, she assured me she was extremely happy working in the Laundry Shop, because it was another old-fashioned friendly firm - and - 'I know most of my customers by name - a lot of them are local people I grew up with.' She does regret however the recent changes in the town, and the loss of 'all the little shops.'

Now we come to a shop which was started 21 years ago 'just for fun', after an unsuccessful attempt at market gardening in Duddenhoe End.

It was because No.1 Emson Close was empty, and Joan Sanderson had been familiar with handicrafts all her life, that she decided to open a handicraft shop. Now Colorcraft is so much a part of Saffron Walden it is almost as if it has always been in the town.

It would be impossible to list all the different types of handicrafts covered by Colorcraft, not to mention the comprehensive stock of artists' materials also sold. So it comes as no surprise to learn that Joan Sanderson's customers come from all over Essex, including the London area, as well as places like Huntingdon, Bedford and Bury St. Edmunds.

Joan herself is one of those incredible people who can manage to do at least three things at once. One minute she and the customer she is serving are both down on their hands and knees on the shop floor with Joan carefully measuring and cutting off lengths of something. Next minute she's foraging for some brick-printed paper for the outside of a doll's house. And all the time she is answering questions, telling her assistant just where to look for that particular tapestry, embroidery silk, bead fastener or fabric paint.

She is also an expert interpreter and seems to know exactly what her customers are looking for, even though they themselves have only the vaguest idea. If she doesn't stock whatever it is, then she will tell them where they will be able to buy it. It is small wonder therefore that visitors who make Saffron Walden an annual pilgrimage, always include a visit to Colorcraft as part of it.

Leaving Colorcraft and the shops in Emson Close we now reach one of the oldest and most historic parts of town, The

The Cockpit with old Town Maltings in the background.

Cockpit. For those of us who dislike cruel sports, the name of this tiny narrow (and quite often odorous) passage, hardly conjures up thoughts of "Merry England." But from about the 12th century until the middle of the 19th century The Cockpit in Saffron Walden must have flourished, standing as it does, immediately behind the Market Place. Thankfully it is now perpetuated only by name.

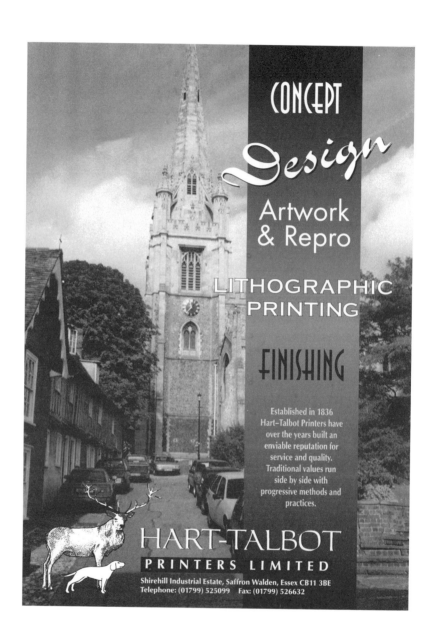
136

CHAPTER FIVE

Market Hill

First published in the Saffron Walden Weekly News
June 7 – July 19, 1990

In the early 17th century Market Hill was a continuation of Market Lane (King Street), a narrow turning off the High Street which continued into the Market Place, and up the hill. But by 1840 Market Lane had become Market End Street, the lower part of the hill - Market End - and the upper part near to the Sun Inn - Sun Hill. Later, between 1840 and 1851 the name - Market Hill - appears to have become accepted.

Number 1 Market Hill is described in Department of Environment notes as an "early 19th century stucco fronted building". But it will be remembered by many as, a shop called Pennings. There was no shop quite like Pennings the grocers!

In August 1980 I wrote in the Saffron Walden Weekly News - "There is a comforting timelessness about Pennings. It is a pleasant thought that the present proprietors, Leslie and James Penning, sons of the original owner, John Francis Penning, intend to keep it that way."

And they did too - right up to the moment they gave the final tug on the rope, which had opened and closed their door for so many years. The final tug came in September 1986.

Outwardly there was little to command the attention. But to enter the shop just once was enough to inscribe it indelibly on the memory. There was always a nostalgic perfume of freshly ground coffee, tea, spice, cheese and other exciting scents. Scents now associated with a more

Leslie (right) and Jim (left) Penning in their grocer's shop at No. 1 Market Hill.

leisured, less frenetic age than ours.

You crossed the threshold and entered into a lost world, to a time before the age of pre-packaging, when sugar came in thick blue paper bags; ham was cut from the bone; bacon sliced to the thickness of the customer's preference; cheese cut from the round and coffee ground whilst you waited. It was an experience to be savoured and cherished.

That this atmosphere managed to exist right up to the middle of the 1980s is due entirely to the attitude of the two brothers who ran the business. Their father had instilled in them all the attitudes of a good old-fashioned grocer, with the result that to the very end the shop was always never less than crowded.

John Francis Penning, a local boy, began working for John Stebbing Leverett as an errand boy soon after the first World War. Leverett was a man of considerable substance. His family had been in business in Walden for many generations and appears in the earliest rating lists for the town on this site.

The 1851 Census List gives the name John Leverett "Mayor, Draper and Grocer." It was he, whose full name was John Wycliffe Leverett, who demolished the original shop (or office) on this site, and rebuilt it with the addition of a warehouse at the back. (His initials J.W.L. 1849 are still to be seen on the warehouse wall at the rear of the shop.)

According to rating lists, he appears to have owned all the premises on western side of Market Hill as far as the Green Dragon (Trustee Savings Bank). Possibly he died about 1862 because his son's name - Stebbing Leverett - appears in the rating lists for that year against that of "the late John Leverett".

Stebbing Leverett, like his father, was a man of enterprise. Rating lists show that not only did he have shops in Market Hill but also across the way in Market Place in the building which was later to become Emson Tanner's, and also adding "undertaking" to his list of services.

But glancing at old rating lists, it looks as if his early achievements began to decline and by the turn of the century his enterprises have dwindled and his son John Stebbing Leverett is running the business which was later to employ young John Francis Penning.

In the late 1920s John Penning bought the shop from his old employer and continued the business on his own account with a staff of four assistants.

This was the time when people from the outlying districts came into Walden to do their shopping by horse and trap. The horses and traps would stop outside the shop in the corner of the Market Place, and young John Penning would come out, order book in hand, to take down the customer's order whilst she remained seated in her trap.

But gradually as the decade progressed the horses and traps disappeared and customers from the surrounding villages no longer came personally to collect their orders. Instead John Penning would send out a boy on a bike, sometimes as far as Ickleton and Walden Pond Street to collect the orders which would be delivered by the same boy next day.

In 1945 however, the boy on the bike gave way to a small Morris van driven by a young lady called Joyce Nicholson. With the passing years the van increased in size and so did the number of Pennings' customers, for now the children of the children of John Penning's early customers were following their parents' example. Also, the number of village shops was declining, as were the delivery services offered by the larger grocery chains.

Pennings remained unique to the end, and many elderly village people have great cause to regret its passing.

The closing of Pennings made local history - their customers gathered in the Town Library to present them with gifts and drink their health - and the whole thing was televised!

For many months the shop stood empty and forlorn - like its close neighbour - and then just before Christmas 1987, the shop in the corner of the Market Place opened its doors once again to Saffron Walden. Windows which once displayed high-class food products are now filled with a handsome collection of jewellery, both modern and antique, Elizabeth Michael has arrived!

Elizabeth and her partner Michael (surnames they say are irrelevant) specialise in top-class hand-made modern jewellery, and unusual, well-made antique jewellery. They also design settings for customer's own stones, or a piece of jewellery especially for them.

Stebbing Leverett's shop, Market Hill – 1930.

Elizabeth, whose grandfather was a jeweller, grew up in the jewellery trade and is a fount of knowledge on the subject. So is manageress Julie Reed who, although having had no formal training, 'just loves jewellery', and has learnt everything she knows from 'Beth and Mick and talking to dealers.'

Former customers of Pennings who venture over the threshold of Elizabeth Michael are delighted to find a reminder of the old days - the original wooden shelving painted white and the marble from the cheese and bacon counter just where it always was. But what happened to the rope pull which opened the door? No-one seems to know!

Next door to Pennings was a drapery business which continued to trade under the name, Stebbing Leverett & Sons until the 1950s when it became Dormie's menswear shop. This in turn became the ladies' dress shop Eurostyle.

——— • ———

Department of Environment Notes describe No.5 Market Hill as "an early 19th century grey gault brick building". Yet it is common knowledge that this was the site of the Green Dragon Inn, which appears in records as early as 1757. Does this mean that the inn was pulled down and rebuilt at sometime?

The Green Dragon continued to function as an inn until about 1934, when the local magistrates refused to renew the licence on the grounds that there were too many inns in the area of the Market Place. The sign was then transferred to a beerhouse called 'the Butcher's Arms' at Sewards End, and the Market Hill premises taken over by Mr. Teddy Warley - Saddler of Cates Corner.

In the early 1950s the premises again changed hands and became the Cambridge & District Trustee Savings Bank.

Although No.5 is still the home of the T.S.B., the original image of the small savers's bank has been completely swept away since its recent floatation. In its place is a highly computerised organisation with, 'what must be the best computer system of all the banks in the country', according to Manager, Paul Grant.

Even the old building itself has undergone a face-lift, substituting its cosy old character with cool, modern sophistication.

Next door, at No.7, we find one of those shops colloquially known as a "Charity Shop" which, in recent years have sprung up in all towns. The Imperial Cancer Research Fund shop specialises in selling good quality second-hand clothing for men, women and children, plus books, jewellery and bric-a-brac.

Many people will remember No.7 as part of Chisnall's grocery and delicatessen. The older generation will perhaps recall when the shop belonged to the Sawyers. But how many know that this was the original "Cro's Stores"? That it was here that Benjamin Cro set up his business in 1885, later, at the turn of the century, moving to Nos.27 & 29 High Street?

Crossing over to the east side of Market Hill we see the elegant side door of Eaden Lilley surmounted by a carved wooden head, believed to be a likeness of John Emson.

John Emson was the miller turned shop-keeper who added certain refinements to this already handsome building in the early 19th century, his name to be perpetuated when the Tanner family took over the business at the turn of the century. (See Market Place).

The next building, Winstanley House, is described by Department of Environment Notes as "a 17th century timber-framed and plastered building with a long wing extending east into the Cockpit and a gable end at the west end on Market Hill with a jettied upper storey. A small wing extends northwards up Market Hill..."

Winstanley House is so called because it is believed to have been the birthplace of Henry Winstanley, born in Saffron Walden in 1644.

It has been said that Henry Winstanley was a mixture of engineer, artist, entrepreneur and conjuror. In his twenties he was Clerk of Works at Audley End and on his marriage built a house at Littlebury filled with practical jokes. (This house is now alas, demolished.)

He was a talented engraver and wellknown for his famous views of Audley End House, and pack of playing cards which he designed and published about 1670.

142

His theatre - Winstanley's Waterworks – which stood close to what we now know as Hyde Park Corner in London, was filled with effects in fire and water and was the sensation of its age.

Later on in his life he became involved in the shipping trade, and it was the foundering of two of his vessels on the Eddystone Rocks, which prompted him to design and build the first Eddystone Lighthouse in 1699.

The lighthouse was made of wood, and doubts were expressed as to its strength. Henry, whose wish it was to be on the ligthouse during a severe storm, strongly refuted these doubts, and had the pleasure of his wish being granted in November 1703 when he and his workmen were attending to the maintenance of the light and a violent storm arose. The storm, believed to have been the worst that ever struck Southern England, cost the lives of 8,000 people, including Henry Winstanley. He vanished, like his lighthouse, into the stormy depths without trace.

Next door to Winstanley House - the Chinese Restaurant "Chef Peking" - a handsome three-storey building, has Georgian pediments to french windows opening on to a delicate wrought-iron balcony on the first floor.

Market Hill east side.

143

Many people will remember this early 19th century building, as Mr. Cresswell's Chemist's shop. E.P. Cresswell was carrying on a long-established tradition at No.6 Market Hill. And if you stand at the bottom of the Hill you can still see the old advertisement of a previous chemist, Walter Harrison Scott, who ran his business here in 1913.

Rating lists show that from 1833 - and probably earlier - a long line of chemists operated from these premises, the first one recorded being Jeptha Miller.

Across the road are Nos. 9 - 11 Market Hill, described by Department of Environment notes as "An 18th century timber-framed and stuccoed building possibly incorporating an earlier medieval building."

Mr. Barry Tyler of Tyler Insurance, set up his Insurance Broking business here in 1984, after spending a year restoring the place. He told me that the building is believed to date from about 1450, (No.11) with a later 18th century addition (No.9). The northern wall of No.9 being the original exterior wall of No.11.

Mr. Tyler admitted that when he bought the property, which was more or less derelict, he found the prospect of

Members of the Cork Club outside the King's Arms – 1930.

144

restoring it frightening. However, now that the roof no longer leaks and the crumbling walls have been renovated, he says he has a great feeling of satisfaction.

Mr. Tyler has retained as many of the building's original features as possible, including exposing and covering with glass, some of the original lath and plaster of what was the exterior wall of No.11. He said that No.11 was almost certainly a medieval shop, with goods sold from a stall set up outside, and that the upper storey would have overhung the pavement. At some time, the lower storey had been built out flush with the upper storey, thus making a legal encroachment onto the pavement. That is why the property is out of line with its next door neighbour No.13.

But again, many people will remember No.9 and 11 Market Hill, as part of Chisnall's Grocery and Delicatessen shop, and Lambert's Greengrocery.

——— • ———

Once Market Hill boasted three pubs - the Green Dragon, the Sun Inn and the King's Arms - now it has only one - the King's Arms.

The King's Arms, described by Department of Environment Notes as "an early 19th century grey gault brick front to a l6th/l7th century timber-framed building," has been traced back as far as 5th September 1681. At that time it was called "John Turner's Plow", later, in 1736, "The Post Horses" and from 1740 onwards "the King's Arms."

There is a theory that, centuries ago, the name "the King's Arms" was given to any inn run by a retired service man. Whether this applies to the change of name in this instance must be a matter of conjecture. Certainly the inn displays evidence of having been an old coaching inn, because "yard, stables and coach house" are recorded in the rating lists for 1790.

The stables were still used in 1929 and later, when people from the surrounding villages still came into Saffron Walden by pony and trap. Mrs. Elsie Lines of Goddard's Way, told me that her father, Mr. Ernest Dyer, landlord of the King's Arms at that time, employed an ostler to feed, water and stable the ponies, and look after the traps, for which, a fee of 3d (1¹/2p) was charged. As times changed and cars took over from horses, some of the stables were turned into lock-up garages.

Many people also cycled into town, and here again, they could leave their bikes for 2d (1p) the whole day in a shed (probably the old coach house) at the King's Arms.

Ernest and Annie Dyer were dairy farmers in Cheshunt, but by the 1920s Ernest felt he would prefer running a pub instead. A friend told him that the landlord of the King's Arms - Mr. Chapman - was about to retire and suggested he go and see him. That was how the Dyer family, Ernest, Annie, and their three children Annie, Ernest and Elsie, came to live at the King's Arms in 1929.

In those days the inn was very different to what it is now, and the Dyer family only had electricity downstairs, it was a case of "to bed with a candle" at the end of the day. But the inn enjoyed a good reputation for accommodation, and was very popular with lorry drivers and commercial travellers. For 3/6d (21p) a night, they could have a bed, a home-cooked supper and a good old-fashioned full English breakfast.

Elsie's husband, Mr. Ted Lines, told me that as a young airman in the regular Airforce in the 1930s, he bought a round of drinks in the King's Arms - 17 whiskies, 3 half pints of mild and bitter, and 3 half pints of mild - and the total cost of the round came to 11/4¹/2d (about 67p).

He added - 'you could get drunk on half-a-crown (12¹/2p) and still have enough for your bus fare home!'

Elsie, who went to South Road School, later trained to be a shorthand typist-bookkeeper. For many years she worked in the office at Raynham's Garage, playing the piano in the pub in the evenings, 'because that was the only form of entertainment in a pub in those days'. That is how she and Ted met.

They married and moved away, but during the second World War, Elsie often came back to the King's Arms to help her parents. Later, when Ted finally retired from the Airforce, they took on another local pub in the town - the Queen Elizabeth - which they ran for nearly 31 years.

146

It was Elsie's parents who - persuaded by some of their regulars - started the "Cork Club" at the King's Arms. This was about 1933. Membership was for men only, and each member paid 2d a week. Members had to carry with them, at all times, a cork studded with brass nails at each end.

When one member met another member outside the pub, one would challenge the other, by saying 'have you got your cork?' The other man would then tap his cork, to prove that he had. If the man challenged hadn't got his cork on him, he had to pay a fine of 3d towards the Club funds. The funds were used for social occasions and outings, 'usually to Southend-on-Sea'.

The Club had a very large membership, and Mrs. Dyer, crocheted each member a blue and white tie, which they all wore on the various outings. But, like so many such institutions, the second World War saw the demise of the Cork Club at the King's Arms.

During their time at the King's Arms, Mr. and Mrs. Dyer made various improvements to the building and in doing so, uncovered many interesting features. One was the opening up of a doorway which had been sealed, perhaps for centuries, and which revealed a stairway leading down the side of the cellar and out to a tunnel at the back, which they assumed led to the old Castle.

Another feature, was the discovery of two tiny attic rooms above the kitchen. There was no means of entering either room apart from two little windows which looked out onto the yard. By this means the rooms were eventually entered and made into one.

Mr. and Mrs. Dyer finally retired in 1947, after 18 years in a trade which had changed considerably since they first took over in 1929.

The present landlord of the King's Arms, Mr. Jack de Lee took over in 1967, and proudly boasts that he is the second longest serving Landlord in the town. (Mr. Jordan at the Railway Arms is the longest).

As a director and general manager of a group of garages in Wanstead, he longed for independence and above all, to get away from the rat race. And like a lot of men, he fancied running a pub.

The King's Arms offered him exactly the sort of accommodation he and his wife, Helen, were looking for, big enough to accommodate their three children and Jack's mother.

Now the children are grown-up and married and sadly, Helen died eight years ago. But Mrs. Rita de Lee, Jack's mother, a lively 95 year-old lady who does her own shopping and cooking, is very much in command at the King's Arms.

Over the years Jack de Lee has also renovated the old inn, trying, wherever possible to reveal the best features of its antiquity. It took him a year to clean and scrape the old beams. He also removed old plaster from one wall to expose the timber-framing, discovering two skeletons of what he believes must have been squirrels, plus a quantity of nutshells.

He also found the original old fireplace, with what might have been a bake-oven and hooks in the chimney, probably used for smoking hams, and exposed some of the original Elizabethan bricks in the chimney breast.

Jack has decided ideas on how a pub should be run. He will not allow gaming machines, pool tables or juke boxes

Jack de Lee,
Landlord of the King's Arms – 1990.

on his premises, and says 'I look after an endangered species - people who come into a pub for a drink and a chat!'

He admits that the anti drink and drive campaign has affected his trade but 'no more than any other pub. If people do go over the top, they can leave their car here in my car park, and this is something which I encourage them to do.'

Reminiscing about the past, he recalls the night of the fire at the Rose & Crown. Most of the survivors were brought to the King's Arms first, and Jack and Helen worked all night, making hot drinks, providing clothing and doing their very best to make them comfortable. 'In the end we made so many hot drinks and sandwiches, that we ran out of tea, coffee, milk, bread - practically everything.'

But he does feel extremely bitter - understandably - about being misquoted in the national press when asked 'how long did it take for the fire engines to get to the scene of the fire?' Jack replied - 'I don't know - in an emergency a minute seems like an hour!' A remark which appeared in some newspapers as 'the local fire brigade took an hour to get to the fire!'

Over the years the King's Arms has been a popular venue for local farmers' meetings, including the Young Farmers Club, and Jack himself was chairman of the Local Rugby Club for 16 years.

But Jack de Lee is a man of varied interests, for one thing he is an extremely competent artist. 'Destined,' he says, 'to become a commercial artist after I left school, but unfortunately the second World War intervened.'

Mostly he sketches with a biro, and enjoys drawing plants and flowers. He also appreciates other artists' work and has a splendid collection of drawings and paintings by local artists.

His other great interest is wine. This shows in the extensive wine list at the King's Arms, which includes many wines not easily obtainable elsewhere.

It is quite obvious Jack enjoys his way of life, and his role of mine host. When asked if he has any especially interesting customers, he replies 'all my customers are interesting!'

But when asked about the ghost, said to haunt one of the bedrooms of the King's Arms - a cold clammy presence which pulls the bedclothes of any one sleeping in that room - Jack de Lee gives a knowing look and says - 'any pub landlord will find you a ghost - it's good for trade!'

——— • ———

According to Department of Environment notes, No. 13 Market Hill - Hamptons Estate Agents - dates back to the early 19th century. So we may assume that when Gibson & Co. opened their Saffron Walden and North Essex Bank on this site, the premises were purpose-built and to this very day, the original safe belonging to the Bank, remains in situ at No.13 - now known as Gibson House.

As we have learned before (Chapter One - Market Place) the Saffron Walden and North Essex Bank was opened in 1824 to defy the Searle family - the very first Bankers in Saffron Walden - who unfortunately set up as malsters in opposition to the Gibsons. This competition resulted in the collapse of the Searle Bank in 1825.

The Gibson Bank flourished in Market Hill until 1874 when it moved to a new and splendidly ornate building in the Market Place. During the decades which followed the Bank changed its name several times as a result of various mergers until ultimately it became what we know now as "Barclays Bank".

Meanwhile No.13 Market Hill became The General Post Office - postmaster William Spicer - until it moved in 1890 to King Street (now W. H. Smith).

After that, No.13 - still owned by the Gibson family - enjoyed a series of tenants, most of them, ladies whose profession was either millinery or dressmaking. In 1987 however the London estate agents, Hamptons, took over the premises, with Mr. Bruce Munro and Mr. Michael Snow as joint Regional Directors.

Bruce Munro is very much a local man, born in Thaxted. He started his career, on the advice of his father, with the old established local Estate Agents, Cheffins, in 1950.

One of his very first jobs as a trainee estate agent was to collect the rents from the many small cottages in streets like Castle Street, Bridge End and Pleasant Valley. He describes them as 'primitive little places with outside lavatories, occupied by the same families for generation upon generation. The rents averaging between 3/6d (16p) and 7/6d (40p).'

This was about 40 years ago. Now look in the window of Hamptons and there, amongst the photographs of prestigious dwellings and picturesque country cottages, you will see some of very same tiny cottages offered for sale at an average price of roughly £70,000!

In 1960 Bruce Munro joined Jennings. Mr. Ernest Jennings came to Walden in 1906, taking over an already established business from Mr. Slocombe at No.5 Cross Street. (Down Your Street - Part Two - page 161). For the next 50 years Ernest Jennings, auctioneer and estate agent, became part of the established way of life in the town. He died in 1956.

In 1974 Jennings merged with Sworders, another local estate agent, and in the late 70s moved to No.13 King Street. In 1983 Bruce Munro 'took the Jennings business from

Local estate agent Bruce Munro with staff and friends celebrating in Market Hill – 1988.

Sworders, and called it Sworder Jennings because I remained a partner in the Sworder Suffolk business.' A year later surveyer, Michael Snow of Thaxted joined partnership in Sworder Jennings. Later, in 1987 they sold out to Hamptons and moved to Gibson House on Market Hill.

Next door to Hamptons is part of Lankester Antiques, but for a great many local people this will be remembered for all time as "the Cromwell Cafe".

The Cromwell Tea-rooms (cafe) came into being, I am told, in the 1920s, and were run by a Mrs. Arnold and her daughters. It was here, on market days, that weary farmers' wives would refresh themselves after a day's shopping, before going to seek out their husbands at the Rose & Crown or the Hoops.

But the Cromwell Cafe (or Tea-rooms) has long since disappeared from the local scene, along with the way of life it epitomized - cosy, predictable and unhurried.

——— • ———

Numbers 12 and 14 Market Hill, are really all one 15th century timbered Hall House, according to Department of Environment notes.

The notes list as further interesting features, No.14's early 19th century 3-light double-hung sash window without glazing bars. And No.12's early 19th century shallow, bow shop window with glazing bars and 20th century shop window in early 19th century style. Both have interior exposed timber-framing and 17th century panelling.

These two buildings form a picturesque group, No.12 looking out onto Market Hill as it does, and No.14 a cornerstone to the medieval crossroads, so much a feature of this part of town.

It was quite disturbing - not the least to say shocking - to learn that Nos. 12 and 14 were bought by a local solicitor, just before World War two, with the idea of demolishing them and redeveloping the site. Thankfully the advent of the war saved this valuable architectural contribution to Saffron Walden's history.

Mr. Dick Selves outside his former home in Market Hill.

Mr. Dick Selves of Ashdon Road gave me this incredible peace of information.

Dick was born at No.12 Market Hill 78 years ago (now Mr. Porter's electrical shop). His parents, Richard and Maud Selves, moved from Colchester to Walden, in 1910 when Richard, an employee of the Avery Scale and Weighing Machine Company, set up business on his own account in Market Hill.

Later he was joined by young Dick, who left The Boys' British School in 1926. A year later, Dick also joined the local Fire Brigade, starting off as a "boy messenger."

When his father sold out to Avery in 1945, Dick was employed by Avery and stayed with the firm until he retired in 1976.

Recalling his memories of Market Hill in the early decades of this century, Dick told me that the first of his recollections

Looking down Market Hill at the turn of the century.

was, Mr. Freddie Bird the antique dealer at No.14. After that the business became a ladies' hairdressers run by Mr. Billy Jeffrey.

Old rating lists show that No.14 was a retail outlet of various types for many years. Thomas Coleman - fruiterer - had the premises prior to Mr. Bird, and George Day - clothier - had his shop at No.14 Market Hill from 1856 until 1895. Earlier still, Thomas Branch the shoemaker, was at No.14 from 1840 until 1856.

Dick grew up in the era of horse-drawn traffic and he remembers the horses and carts stopping outside the shop. And watching the soldiers grooming their horses, stabled at the King's Arms, during the first World War.

'Then there were the Horse Sales. They used to run the horses up and down Church Street, with the horses looking lovely, tails and manes plaited and braided.

What was the Cromwell Cafe (Lankester Antiques) was the home of Mr. Isaac Marking senior and his wife.

Our own premises, of course, used to be Hardwick's the fishmongers.'

This information is borne out by old rating lists which reveal that Thomas Hardwick set up business at No.12 Market Hill in 1800, manufacturing mineral waters, pickles and sauces, as well as selling fish and fruit.

He died around 1872, when the business, still run by the family, was transferred to No.9 King Street (now Burtons the Butchers.) (Down Your Street - Part One - page 73). Later, William Armstrong, the watchmaker, came to No. 12 in 1885, and continued for the next 25 years, until Richard Selves took over.

Dick Selves left Market Hill in 1934 when he married Margaret Bass from Debden. They moved to No.17 Ashdon Road, where he still lives. Sadly, Margaret died shortly after Dick retired, nevertheless Dick is blessed with a married daughter, six grand children and four great-grand-children.

CHAPTER SIX

Bridge Street

First published in the Saffron Walden Weekly News
September 6 – November 1, 1990

Many people still refer to Bridge Street as Bridge End, which, according to C.B. Rowntree (Saffron Walden Then and Now) was the early name given to this northern limit of the town. The name is derived from the footbridge across the Madgate Slade before it was bridged over in 1832, later, to be reconstructed in 1967 after heavy floods.

Severe flooding after periods of heavy rain has always been a feature of this part of Saffron Walden. John Player, writing in 1844 in his "Sketches in Essex" gives a vivid account of numerous floods. These are augmented by the experiences of people living in and around Bridge Street during recent years.

Someone who remembers being flooded twice whilst living in Bridge Street is Mrs. Jane Hatton, who lived at Swan Lodge from 1952 until 1974. Mrs. Hatton's husband, the late John Hatton, was Steward of Audley End Estate, during that time.

Swan Lodge, described in Department of Environment notes as "an early-mid 19th century flint walled lodge," is one of the six gateways into Audley End Park. But Mrs. Hatton believes that the house must be much older than the 19th century.

Her support for this theory lies in correspondence which she and her husband found whilst living at Swan Lodge. This correspondence, dating from the early 18th century, related to complaints received by the Estate from close

157

Bridge End – 1850.

neighbours, inferring that the woman living at the Lodge was keeping a "Bawdy House".

In those days Windmill Hill, which leads into Bridge Street was a "drovers road", and so it is quite feasible to suppose that the drovers stopped off at Swan Lodge either coming or going into the town, for a little relaxation!

Swan Lodge itself is a very large five bedroomed residence, which at sometime was divided into two dwellings. Mr. and Mrs. Hatton, their three boys and a lady ghost lived in that part of the house with overlooks the golf course.

Jane Hatton assured me that the ghost was extremely nice and they were all very fond of her. Although she herself never saw the lady full face, she did, on occasions get fleeting glances of her. But her second son, husband and a guest all saw the ghost on different occasions, and all described her as being 'tall, with a brownish coloured dress made of rather coarse material, buttoned down the front, and hair done up in loops over her ears.'

On making enquiries about previous occupants of the Lodge, the Hattons were told that at one time, during the

19th century a gamekeeper and his daughter lived there. The daughter eventually married when she was 40 or thereabouts, and unfortunately died in childbirth. So they assumed that their ghost was the restless spirit of the gamekeeper's daughter, partly because the ages seemed to tally, and partly because the ghost appeared to be very concerned about children.

'There was a door in the kitchen which led to the stairs, and sometimes we would hear the latch of this door being lifted, then footsteps going up the stairs, and someone breathing very audibly on the landing - always outside the children's room,' says Mrs. Hatton.

'Once,' she continues, 'when my husband was ill, I was sleeping in the spare bedroom, and I was awoken by someone pressing very gently on the bedclothes. I took no notice, until the pressure increased and eventually became unbearable. In desperation I got up and went downstairs to find my husband sprawled out on the kitchen floor. His heavy cold had turned into pneumonia. I have always felt that she was warning me.'

Swan Lodge.

159

Mrs. Hatton's story of the friendly family ghost was both convincing and entertaining, and I wondered what had happened to the lady in brown after their departure. With this in mind I contacted Mr. Alan Lofthouse, Green-keeper at the Golf Club, and now the tenant of that part of Swan Lodge once occupied by the Hattons.

Mr. Lofthouse, a committed christian, assured me that his part of the house was not in the least bit haunted. When he took up his position as Green-keeper with Saffron Walden Golf Club almost two and a half years ago, he had the house blessed by a local clergyman. Not because he thought it was haunted but because he wanted the Lord to bless the place where he lived.

—— • ——

"Numbers 1 - 33 (Bridge Street) Bridge End Cottage, Numbers 8, 12, 24 to 32, Eight Bells Inn, Bridge End Farmhouse and Barn, and No.1 Myddylton Place, and the Corner House Freshwell Street form an outstanding group of mainly 15th and 17th century timber-framed buildings."

This is the description given to this part of Saffron Walden by the Department of Environment in their Notes on Ancient Buildings. But despite this rich heritage, if the plans for the Swan Meadow Car Park scheme go ahead, these buildings will bear the brunt of this major upheaval.

Bridge End Cottage (Nos.31 and 33) is believed to be a 15th century timber-framed house, altered in the 16th and 17th centuries. No.31 was also the home of Chief Constable William Campling, murdered by Benjamin Pettit, on the night of 31st October 1849.

Pettit had a grudge against Campling who had brought him to justice for previous offences. On the day he shot Campling, Pettit had been drinking heavily in the Waggon and Horses in Castle Street (later known as the Five Bells) now a private residence called "The Bell House".

At about 9.00pm Pettit borrowed one of the landlord's guns, crossed a field at the back of the Waggon and Horses and dropped down over a wall into the ornamental gardens owned by Francis Gibson. By following the course of the

Slade he made his way to Bridge End where he lay in wait for Campling who was drinking in the Eight Bells.

Campling left the Eight Bells at ten minutes past 10pm and stood talking with an acquaintance - William Brand - for a short while, who then walked as far as Campling's front door with him. Campling was in the act of opening the door when he was shot in the legs. He immediately suspected Pettit, who had threatened him on many occasions, and suggested to Brand that he find out where Pettit was. Later, Campling died of his wounds.

Meanwhile, Pettit had fled, running along the course of the Slade - so as not to leave footprints - to his own house in nearby Almshouse Lane (Park Lane). By 11.30 that same night he was once again seen drinking in the Waggon and Horses, having returned the landlord's gun without being detected. But on his return journey home, via Castle Street, Market Hill, King Street and Almshouse Lane he was unaware that he was being followed by a solicitor's clerk who managed eventually to detain Pettit in conversation until the arrival of a constable.

Pettit was tried at Chelmsford Assizes in March 1850, and despite the evidence of 21 witnesses, nothing conclusive was found against him and the Jury returned a verdict of 'Not Guilty' after retiring for only a quarter of an hour. But there still remained a general opinion in the town that Pettit was guilty, and even today that opinion still prevails.

The Eight Bells itself is undoubtedly one of the most attractive buildings in this street of attractive buildings, dating as it does from the late 16th century, and said to be originally a wealthy Yeoman's home.

It appears to have become a public house about 1840. This was after the Eight Bells in Hill Street was demolished in 1831 to make way for the Borough Market (now the site of Waitrose). (Down Your Street - Part Two - pages 117-119). However, the sign which we see today is not the original one, but one taken from a public house in London during the course of demolition.

The Eight Bells was owned by Francis Gibson and the first landlord was - according to rating lists - William Perkins. An Ordnance Survey Map of 1877 shows the building flanked by two large malthouses, again - according to rating lists - owned by Francis Gibson.

For many years the well-known local family of Pitstow were, at various times, licencees during the 19th century. The last one to be recorded in the rating lists being Selina Pitstow - a lady, it is said, of formidable character. But since those days this fine old building has changed hands many times.

The Eight Bells at the turn of the century.

Francis Gibson, born 1805, grandson of George Gibson founder of the Gibson dynasty in Saffron Walden during the mid-18th century, was less concerned with business matters than the rest of his family. Nevertheless, despite a strong leaning towards the visual arts, he did purchase considerable land and property at the northern end of the town, including Bridge End Farm.

Bridge End Farm is described in Department of Environment notes as an "early 19th century timber-framed and plastered house with an L-shaped plan, renovated in the early 20th century." The Barn - also a listed building - is dated as 17th/18th century, which prompts the supposition that there was an earlier farmhouse on this site.

Bridge End Farm is still very much a working farm, the actual farmhouse now rented out.

Some of the land Francis acquired, was behind the houses of Castle Street on the northern side. It was here, in the 1840s, he created a delightful walled garden, now known as Bridge End Gardens, worthy enough to be now recorded in the Register of Parks and Gardens of Special Historic Interest in England.

A small formal Dutch Garden formed the nucleus, with additional Rose, Fruit and Vegetable gardens, plus an Italianate style maze. This latter, vandalised in previous years, has now been replanted and the paths re-laid, and it is hoped that it will be officially opened to the public next summer as a contribution to "The Year of The Maze" which is to be a national event.

It is said that it was Francis Gibson's intention to construct a tunnel from The Close - his house in the High Street - (See Down Your Street - Part One - pages 1-3) to the Gardens, but whether this was actually started or not we do not know, but certainly it was never completed.

A view through the arch in Bridge End Gardens.

The Gardens are a delight to visit, and contain many interesting features such as the Baroque red brick pavilion, with domed roof and small glazed cupola, to be found close to Bridge Street entrance. And another interesting little pavilion - an octagonal summer house - again with a lead domed roof. This has an interior with an ornamental tiled floor and a cornice with a frieze inscribed to the memory of Francis Gibson.

It is just about here, that the ghost of a lady in white has been seen walking on occasions. But I must add, that there is some doubt as to the authenticity of this story. Nevertheless, I have been told that two different people on two different occasions claim to have seen the ghost.

Another important feature, as yet in need of restoration, is the little fountain in the centre of the Dutch Garden.

Mr. Ben Smeeden, Landscape Architect for Uttlesford District Council, assured me that this is a long-term project because quite a lot of research is being done into the history of the fountain. He believes that the fountain was perhaps damaged at some time, and what we see now is an "ad hoc" version of the original. And he is anxious to ensure that the restoration follows the original design as closely as possible.

Earlier this year, a two-year old apple tree was planted in what is known as "the wilderness", thanks to the efforts of Mrs. Mary Whiteman. The apple tree - known as the Gabriel Harvey apple, was created in an orchard behind Gold Street by Dr. Gabriel Harvey in the 16th century. (Down Your Street - Part One - page 131).

A visit to the gardens for many people will, of course, bring back memories of their schooldays. For it was here that, for many years, in the garden which once provided vegetables for Francis Gibson and his family, many enthusiastic and expert gardeners had their first lessons in gardening.

Apart from Bridge End Gardens, Francis Gibson also left behind another contribution to the town's varied history - his tiny Art Gallery - now known as The Fry Art Gallery.

The Gallery stands just outside the Castle Street entrance of Bridge End Gardens and the unobservant could easily walk past the small blue doorway on the right hand side.

Interior of the Fry Art Gallery.

This would be a pity because even if you are not particularly interested in looking at paintings, the Gallery is well worth a visit.

It was built in 1857 to house Francis's own collection of 17th century Dutch paintings. He died two years later and eventually his only daughter Elizabeth, who had married into the Fry family, (the Quaker chocolate makers of Bristol) inherited the property.

Elizabeth's son, Lewis George Fry, inherited his grandfather's artistic talent, and became a notable landscape painter. He also inherited Bridge End Gardens and shortly after the turn of the century opened them to the public. At the same time he allowed access to the Gallery - for those interested - by application to the Head Gardener for the key.

This amenity was continued after his death by his son, Dr. Lewis Salisbury Fry, up until 1972, when the rising cost of insurance and the growing problem of security forced the Fry family to close the Gallery to the public.

For the next fourteen years the small Gallery slowly declined into a sad, gloomy little ghost, empty and forgotten

165

by most people. It might have continued like this, and eventually crumbled into oblivion had it not been for Mrs. Iris Weaver - a member of the "Friends of Bridge End Gardens Society".

She happened to notice it quite by accident when walking in Bridge End Gardens one day. After making inquiries she discovered, that there were others who also felt that the tiny little building should be saved. It was thanks to Iris Weaver and her friends, who contacted Mr. Anthony Fry - the wellknown figure and landscape painter - grandson of Lewis George Fry, that the Art Gallery was re-born.

Arrangements were made for the newly formed "Fry Art Gallery Society" to acquire a lease on the property for 21 years. Then, an extremely active Committee, plus an energetic band of volunteers worked hard to raise funds to refurbish the Gallery.

Now, five years later, this delightful little Gallery has undergone a wonderful transformation. The interior has been cleaned and redecorated, the floor stripped and repolished, the roof and guttering repaired. And although refurbishment is still far from complete, the Gallery was officially opened to the public for the first time on Easter Saturday, 18th April 1987.

It now houses a permanent collection of the works of North West Essex artists who have made a significant contribution to British Art in the 20th century. There is also an extensive collection of paintings and drawings by members of the Fry family, including Lewis George Fry, R.B.A., R.W.A. (1860-1933), Roger Fry, Anthony Fry L.G., R.W.A. and Francis Gibson himself.

The Gallery is open every Saturday and Sunday afternoon from 2.45pm until 5.30pm, from Easter Sunday until the last Sunday afternoon in October, including Bank Holidays, and admission is free - but donations extremely welcome!

From time to time special exhibitions are held at the Gallery, as well as various social events, lectures, private views and concerts, and new members to the Society are always welcome. And it is a sobering thought that this little gem might have been lost forever had it not been for a very dedicated band of people.

Number 32 Bridge Street is the home of Mr. and Mrs. Andy Russell, who, during the six years they have lived here, have lovingly and painstakingly restored this delightful 15th century cottage.

It was during the renovation that an official from Essex County Council dated the property at about 1485 and the extension to the rear as being early 17th century. (This extension has a slate roof, authentic for this type of building). After the official's visit Pat was fired with enthusiasm to look into the early history of this fascinating little cottage.

She started by consulting the old almanacks in the Town Library, plus the 1851 Census List as well as old deeds, and she eventually built up a comprehensive list of the previous occupants of No.32.

Although she admits that her research is far from complete, she discovered that in nearly 200 years the house has had only ten owners - the Russells being the 10th. But for much of this time the property has been let out to tenants - the longest tenancy being 44 years.

She feels convinced that at one time No.32 was a shop of some description, and Andy feels certain that it was probably an inn from the construction of the ground floor rooms. However, old rating lists reveal no evidence that this property was ever a shop or inn, and it is always recorded as "house and garden" or just "house". But ratings lists only go as far back as 1757, and it is quite possible that No.32 could have been a commercial property at sometime. Certainly when the Russells were creating their lovely little garden at the rear of the house, they discovered a great many flints and pieces of stone - including one engraved "J.W. 1814".

The J.W. must have been James Willings who inherited the property from his father Edward Willings in 1814, and Andy has a theory that perhaps James Willings was a stone-mason.

Many people will remember however, the late Miss W. Gatesman who lived at No.32 before the Russells bought it from her executors. Miss Gatesman was a familiar and much loved personality in the town, a retired nurse, who had once worked at the General Hospital in London Road.

Although Pat and Andy love living in their cottage in Bridge Street, they are now reluctantly considering moving to a larger house. Pat's children from a previous marriage, pretty 16 year-old Jo - doing her A-levels at The County High, and 13 year-old Matthew - also at The County High, are growing up. And Matthew is literally growing up! So much so that he now can only stand upright in the cottage if he stands between the beams in the ceiling.

Andy - a freelance Electronic and Computer Product Designer - also works from home, and this also presents a space problem in a different form!

And of course there's Katie and Sophie, two gorgeous bearded Collie dogs - mother and daughter - as well as Thomas O'Malley and Lucky - the Russells' cats. Despite the fact that the cottage is much larger than it looks and has three bedrooms, old world charm presents difficulties!

Undoubtedly Pat and Andy will miss No.32 if they do decide to move, because they love living in this particular part of the town. 'It is so friendly,' says Pat, 'just like a village. And things have improved enormously since they have prohibited large lorries coming down the hill into town. What I can't understand though, is why they allow them to drive up the hill to go out of the town?

This is a conservation area, and very popular with visitors and tourists, especially at weekends. And these centuries-old houses were never built to withstand the effects of extremely heavy traffic.'

Pat's concern is certainly justified, and the fact that she and Andy live in one of the most photographed houses in the town - 'every weekend we get at least one tourist posing for a photograph outside our door' - supports her concern.

Perhaps this is why she worked as secretary for the Swan Meadow Action Group for two years. Like a lot of people she just cannot understand why the authorities are going ahead with a scheme which will ultimately ruin the most historic and picturesque part of the town.

Number 24 Bridge Street, another charming 15th century cottage is the home of Mr. Ron Masters, a Freelance Technical Illustrator.

Ron Masters, born in Ilford, brought his family to live in

Great Sampford in 1955, after they spent an idyllic Easter weekend there with friends. A year later they moved into an almost derelict Manor House and started to renovate it.

'And I naively thought I was going to commute to London from Thaxted Railway Station, ' says Ron. 'Imagine my surprise when, I set off on the first Monday morning and found Thaxted Railway Station was no longer a railway station!'

In 1963 the Masters opened a music shop on the site of what is now Bacons' Greengrocer's shop in King Street. But at that time Saffron Walden was a much smaller town, and there just wasn't enough trade to support a family. Later, in 1967 they moved to 26 Bridge Street, Ron moving next door when he and his wife divorced.

Like No.32, No.24 has been extended - probably in the 16th century - and throughout its long life, it has always been part of the Bridge End Farm complex, still owned, to this day, by the Fry family.

Most people in Bridge Street have experienced severe flooding at times, including Ron. And he remembers vividly when the water rose to a level of five feet in the downstairs rooms during the terrible floods of the 1960s.

Bridge Street in the floods – 1960s.

169

Eighty-five years-old Mrs. Florence Sizer, who lives in Elm Grove, remembers Bridge Street as it was in 1914.

She was nine years old when her parents moved to No.31 Bridge Street to carry on the mineral water business which her grandfather started behind No.31 before the turn of the century. Her father - Alfred Salmon - and his brother -Albert - were "oilmen" and used to travel around in horse-drawn vans selling hardware, and mineral waters.

'We had four horses and vans, and each driver had a young boy to help him,' says Mrs. Sizer. 'It was terribly hard work. The horses had to be fed and seen to first thing in the morning and at the end of each day. And every weekend father would be cleaning out their stables and seeing to their needs.

The stables were in the large yard behind the house, and there was also an enormous manure heap. I have never seen such a big manure heap in all my life. People would come with their wheelbarrows and buy a wheelbarrow full for 6d.

My sister and I were allowed to go into the machinery shed to help wash the bottles. Here there was a huge tub filled with cold water, and we were given bottle brushes with very long handles so that we could get right down into the bottles.

In those days all mineral water bottles had glass "marbles" in the top of the neck. The gas from the mineral water kept the marble in place, and when the bottle was empty the marble fell down into the neck.

I can't remember all the flavours, but I do remember there was raspberry, and lemonade and ginger beer of course. But there was also one flavour which had a light brown coloured label in the shape of a crown - this was called "King's Own." Sticking the labels onto the bottles was another job we were allowed to do, and it made us feel extremely important.'

Ill-health gradually got the better of Alfred Salmon, and the four horse-drawn vans were reduced to two, and then finally he sold out to Robsons, one of the town's premier retailers. (Down Your Street - Part One - page 85). For a great many years after, Robsons continued to use Alfred Salmon's bottles, and even today, empty mineral water

Bridge Street before the timbers of the Youth Hostel were exposed.
Boy in the foreground is the late H. C. Stacey.

bottles may still be found with name Salmon embossed upon them.

Mrs. Sizer recalls Bridge Street in the early days of the century as 'a funny old street, with not many shops. But there was Goddards the Pork Butchers on the Castle Street corner' (now an antique shop), 'and next to it my uncle Mark Salmon's shop No.1 Castle Street' (still there) 'and of course Thomas Barcham's grocer's shop on the corner of Myddlyton Place. Those three shops supplied all our needs.'

After leaving school, young Florence went up to London to work as a cook-general in Service, but later returned to Saffron Walden to act as companion housekeeper to a Mrs. Holland in West Road. Here she stayed until she married.

Her mother had always warned against marrying an "oilman" because 'he would never be at home.' But like a lot of young girls, Florence had a mind of her own and fell in love with Ronald Sizer, who also came from a family of travelling "oilmen". (Down Your Street - Part Two - pages 25-28).

She says it was quite true, her husband did work extremely long hours driving his "Somerlite" Model T Ford van along the highways and byways around Saffron

Walden, but she never regretted it during the whole of their 53 years of happy married life.

We now come to No.19 Bridge Street, the home of Mr. and Mrs. John Close. Mrs. Close - Dorothy - to all her friends, has lived at No.19 Bridge Street since 1945.

She came to No.19 with her first husband - Mr. Joe Dixon. Joe was a Yorkshireman who came to Saffron Walden to find work during the Depression of the 1930s. During the second World War he served in the Royal Artillery, and was left behind at the evacuation of Dunkirk. Taken prisoner by the Germans he escaped, was recaptured, and then once again escaped.

The second time he was successful. After a series of hair-raising adventures - including swimming a cess pit, dressing as a French peasant and bumping into a German Officer on a train (the officer apologised profusely) - he managed to get into Spain via the Pyrenees.

Later, he was awarded the Military Medal 'but he always insisted that he didn't know what for!' says Mrs. Close.

After his sudden death in 1957, Mrs. Close gave her daughter, Josephine, the medal. Unfortunately it was lost when Josephine moved house 14 years ago, and now she would dearly love to get it back. So if anyone reading this ever comes across a World War two Military Medal awarded to Joseph Dixon of the Royal Artillery No.1072726 - perhaps they would let Josephine or her mother know!

After the death of her first husband, Dorothy resigned herself to widowhood, vowing she would never marry again. Although she did remember - with some affection - a nice young man from her girlhood days. His name was John Close, and it so happened that he also had been a prisoner of war - in the Far East.

John was taken prisoner after the fall of Singapore, and remembers vividly working on the notorious Burma Railway. They worked every day of the week for 90 days without a break under the watchful eyes of their Korean guards, who, he says were far worse than any Japanese.

'I am not aggressive by nature,' says John. 'I think that stood me in good stead. I just kept out of trouble, and made

172

jolly sure I wasn't caught stealing anything. Of course we all stole food - we were hungry, living mostly on rice. But the main thing was not to get caught!'

Dorothy met John again when he was working in Bridge End Gardens. And when asked 'did you go into the gardens on purpose to see John?' she gives a mischievous smile and says - 'perhaps!'

They married in 1964 making John 'an instant Dad and an instant Grandad!'

John was made Head Gardener of Bridge End Gardens in 1966 where he worked until he retired in 1979. Although he says firmly that he doesn't believe in ghosts, and has certainly never seen one in the gardens, he does admit that they can be very eerie sometimes. 'Mostly at dusk, and always in the same place, near to the summer house. I never saw anything, it was just a strange eeriness in that part of the gardens.'

Dorothy agrees. 'It is perfectly true - it is nothing you can put your finger on - and it is just in that spot - nowhere else - and only at dusk. During the daytime the gardens are absolutely beautiful, even down by the summer house.'

John chuckles. 'I think there must be two young girls somewhere who are convinced the gardens are haunted though.

One evening, I'd gone to lock up and entered by the Bridge Street gate. A group of youngsters came into the gardens at the same time by the Castle Street entrance. Two of the young girls approached me, unaware that I was there standing in the gloom lighting up a stump of a cigarette. Suddenly they saw me - I suppose I was standing very still puffing out clouds of smoke - and perhaps I did look like a ghost. To my amazement they let out piercing shrieks and fled for their lives.'

Many people will remember Dorothy as one of the assistants at Woolworths in the High Street during those halcyon days when Woolworths sold 'nothing over sixpence'. She was born in East Street and her early memories of East Street are featured in Down Your Street - Part Two - pages 239-240.

Number 15 Bridge Street, officially known as Bridge House, is one of the largest and historically important houses in the Street but whose outward appearance belies its age.

It is recorded by the Department of Environment, as a "16th-17th century timber-framed and plastered house with a fine 16th-17th century brick chimney stack".

In its heyday it must have been splendid, with many outbuildings, a large garden and an orchard. All of which have been sold off in recent years for building development.

In 1790 it was a private residence, then in the early 19th century - around the time of the revival of the silk industry in Saffron Walden - a silk factory.

Grout Bayley or (Baylis) of Bocking were silk manufacturers who - according to Mrs. Dorothy Monteith's Thesis - set up a silk factory in a 16th century house in Bridge Street, Saffron Walden. Grout & Co., later Grout Bayley & Co. rented No.15 - "house and warehouse" from Alderman Thomas Smith from 1814 to 1830. These dates co-incide with the rise and fall of the silk industry in Walden.

By 1851 however, 77 year-old Alderman Smith and his wife were living in Bridge House themselves, and on his death - about 1864 - it was bought by the Gibsons who later sold it to Lord Braybrooke. From 1887 until 1911, John Wilkinson, general draper, lived and ran his business at No.15, eventually buying the property. After 1911, it belonged to Joseph Custerson who, in 1913, rented part or all of it, to the newly formed Independent Labour Party (which held its very first meeting at No.33 South Road in 1913). However, by 1920, Bridge House had once again reverted to a private residence, and has remained so ever since.

No.7 Bridge Street, just a little further along than Bridge House, is a tiny cottage, dating from the late 15th century, and believed to have been part of a larger "hall-house". (Department of Environment Notes link No.5 with No.7).

Mr. and Mrs. Stammers have been living at No.7 for the past 25 years, after Mr. Stammers - a Divisional Foreman for Essex County Council Highways and Bridges Department - retired. Although they both come from the Colchester area, and have only actually lived in Saffron Walden since 1961, they feel that Saffron Walden is their home town.

They both belong to the Methodist Church - Mrs. Stammers is a Committee member of the Woman's Own - and it is through the Church that they have made some very good friends. These friendships have been augmented for Mr. Stammers by others formed on the allotments on Windmill Hill.

A keen gardener, he has had an allotment since 1962, and even at the age of 86 he seldom misses a day 'down on the allotment'. Here a strong brotherhood of fellow gardeners has been formed over the years, where everyone helps everyone else, and fortunate indeed, is the gardener who is allowed to join!

Members of the older generation will recall No.2 Bridge Street as young Tom Goddard's first butchers shop. (See Church Street pages 81-82). It is now an antique shop but, it is interesting to note that, as far back as 1886 this small shop was operating as a pork butcher's run by William Shepherd. And in those days William Shepherd's shop would have been just one of many tiny shops in the street.

——— • ———

The architectural splendour of No.1 Bridge Street, which stands on the corner of Bridge Street and Myddylton Place is described in Department of Environment Notes as "A very important 15th century timber-framed and plastered house." Yet, those familiar with Saffron Walden refer to it simply as - The Youth Hostel.

The early history of this interesting building is rather obscure, but there is a belief that it was once the home of a wealthy merchant - probably connected with the cloth trade. Evidence to support this theory lies in the proximity of Freshwell Street where, in the 14th and 15th centuries the fullers used the springs which abounded there.

Certainly the interior of the building displays all the evidence of wealth - fine oak panelling, carved beams, huge fireplaces and a 17th century tapestry based on a painting by

175

The Youth Hostel today.

the Dutch Artist, Tenier. Unfortunately, in recent years, many of these interesting features have been obliterated, open fireplaces enclosed in wooden surrounds, and fine oak panelling painted over.

Happily one of the finest features of the building remains intact - a large loft-like room with massive timbers rising unhindered to the roof, lit by mullioned windows. This is now one of the main dormitories of the hostel - available for hire out of season. And in fact, was recently used in the filming of a forthcoming new series of "Lovejoy" due to be shown on BBC television later this year.

At sometime in its long history a maltings was added to the house. Probably about the time that George Gibson acquired the property, as early rating lists show that he owned a "house etc., maltings and offices" on this site in 1790.

In 1794 his son, Atkinson Francis Gibson owned the maltings, later inheriting the house on the death of his father. The property continued to remain in the family (later, the Fry family, through marriage) until the 1930s when it was sold to the Society for the Preservation of Ancient Buildings.

During the second World War, it was rented by the Middlesex Education Committee to provide accommodation for evacuees. Then, in 1947 it was purchased by The Youth Hostels Association who later acquired two further adjoining cottages in Myddylton Place. Since when it has become a focal centre for young visitors to the town.

Fortunately, the Youth Hostel Association are fully aware of the architectural gem they own. Everything possible is being done to ensure the upkeep of the fabric of the building as well as sympathetic restoration whenever funds allow.

In the case of the tapestry which was discovered 15 years ago under layers of wallpaper, this was renovated by the National Trust at Blickling Hall. And in time, the appalling paintwork will be removed from the panelling and beams in the Common Room.

Such an interesting old building cries out to be haunted, especially as it is so close to Myddylton House. But a former warden of the Youth Hostel assured me that he had never seen anything faintly resembling a ghost and then added that, there was a certain dormitory that had a peculiar ambiance. People who slept in that dormitory had very disturbed nights, often waking with a feeling there was a "presence" in the room.

Could this be the ghost of the drunken miller's wife?

It seems that many years ago a miller and his wife lived here, and that one night, the miller, being very drunk, removed some of the floor boards just outside the upstairs room where his wife was stacking sacks of flour. When she had finished her work the woman opened the door and fell to her death through the hole in the floor.

It has also been said that her footsteps are frequently heard climbing an iron staircase - long since demolished - on the outside of the building.

CHAPTER SEVEN

Myddylton Place

First published in the Saffron Walden Weekly News
November 8 – November 15, 1990

Listed by the Department of Environment as an area of outstanding architectural and historical importance, Myddylton Place is a microcosm of 18th century elegance and 15th century timbered charm.

It owes its name to William Myddylton who, in 1530 built a fine mansion in Hoggesgrene, the area between Frosshwell Hundred (Freshwell Street) and Daniels or Fullers Lane (Park Lane). (It is believed that the name Hoggesgrene derives from Richard and John Hog who, in the 14th century owned property in this area.)

William Myddylton called his house Hogs Green House (later the name was changed to Myddylton House.) In accordance with William Myddylton's Will, the house was eventually bequeathed to the almshouses by his daughter Agnes Corbett, and sold to provide money for the poor. It was purchased by George Nicholls, Recorder of Walden, who lived in the house until his death in 1605.

However, doubts have arisen as to whether the present Myddylton House on the north side of Myddylton Place is the original mansion. And there has been a suggestion that, the site of nearby Walden Place, was actually the site of William Myddylton's residence.

But the 1851 Census List shows Mary Ann Fiske living at Myddylton House, and Nathanial Catlin - a partner in the Gibson Bank - as living at Walden Place. And it is generally understood that Myddylton House, as we know it, was bought by Thomas Fiske sometime in the 18th century.

Myddylton Place as it used to be.

Department of Environment notes date the building as "probably an early 16th century house built on a Half H plan but added to and altered in the 18th and 19th centuries and completely refaced in yellow gault brick."

There was a time when Myddylton House was said to be haunted by an extremely malevolent spirit. Frequently people who slept in the house complained of unpleasant dreams, always ending with a headless man, wearing 16th century clothes, killing a member of the family. One maidservant said she dreamt she was being held down by the throat whilst someone tried to kill her.

Someone whose family rented the house for a short while in the late l930s tells the following story:-

'My bedroom door - even when securely locked - would be flung open regularly at precisely the time the church clock struck four in the morning. One night I heard something clomping upstairs and I thought it was my dog, and then the door burst open and whatever it was clomped across the room and into a cupboard behind my bed.'

The eldest son of a family who lived there during the

1960s was sitting at his desk in a tiny room at the top of the house late one evening. On hearing footsteps mounting the stairs, he opened the door and saw a headless man on the threshold. The apparition made a lunge for the boy and for a while they wrestled together until the boy managed to push the ghost down the stairs. Later he told his mother - 'I knew I had to throw him down the stairs, otherwise he would have killed me!'

On another occasion, his younger brother awoke one night to see the curtains of his bedroom window part and a translucent disembodied hand fumbling with the window catch. Having opened the window it then drifted over to his bed. The terrified boy fled screaming to his parents' room.

Shortly after this incident it was decided to have the house exorcised and all the unpleasant ghostly incidents ceased at once.

No-one seems to know the origin of these hauntings, what evil deeds occurred in the past to cause such unquiet spirits. But a young curate who lodged at Myddylton House for a short time is reported to have seen the spectre of 'a hanged servant girl'.

One thing is true however - Myddylton House is not haunted now!

Few people can boast that they have lived in the same house for 95 years. But Mr. Frederick Dennis can, because he was born at No.6 Myddylton place in 1895, one of the nine children of Arthur and Liza Dennis.

In those days No.6 was very different to what it is now. There were no modern conveniences, water came from an outside tap in the yard, and the lavatory - shared with another cottage - was a fair distance from the house. And goodness knows how Arthur and Liza managed to fit all their nine children into two bedrooms - plus themselves.

Fred spent nearly all his working life at Engelmann's Nursery, and travelled all over the country exhibiting Engelmann's flowers. His work brought him into contact with many interesting and famous people - including the Duke of Windsor and the King and Queen of Siam.

Fifty years ago last June, he married Florence, a young lady he had known practically all her life. Florence, now 82,

181

Frederick and Florence Dennis in their home at No. 6 Myddylton Place.

had been born in London but raised by her grand-parents in Saffron Walden after the death of her mother. And like many young women of her generation, she went into Service as soon as she left school, first with Mrs. William Bell and later with Miss Tuke. They have one daughter, Mrs. Pauline Hedger and one granddaughter, Lucy Jane aged 11.

Florence and Fred remember Walden when it was a much closer-knit community than it is now. When Castle Street was rough, full of colourful characters like Billy Wimple who used to beat carpets on the Common and clean windows for a living, and Charlie Wright with his donkey and cart who sold sand to the local pubs.

They remember also Mr. Williams the Jobmaster, with his stables in Freshwell Street, who hired out horses and carriages but always made sure there were two horses in the stables ready to pull the fire engine if it were needed.

But the days of the horse-drawn fire engine have gone and with them gas-light and outdoor sanitation. Over the years No.6 Myddylton Place has been modernised. Now Florence and Fred, and their pet tortoise - 45 year-old

Jimmie - (not available for interview having retired for the winter) enjoy all the conveniences of the late 20th century within the walls of 15th century timbered charm.

We now turn our attention to nearby Walden Place. Rating lists for 1757 show James Raymond as owner of Walden Place, later, in the early 19th century it belonged to Nathanial Catlin - partner in the Gibson Bank. (See Market Place, pages 7-8). Later still the son of another partner in the Bank, William Favill Tuke (George Stacey Gibson's nephew) bought Walden Place about 1903 and lived there until 1914.

William Favill Tuke married Eva Knockolds, daughter of Martin Knockolds of Castle Hill. They had one son - Anthony William - and an adopted daughter, Elizabeth, the youngest child of Eva Knockold's sister, who died soon after the child was born. It is thanks to Elizabeth Tuke Jenkins that we have a picture of what life was like at Walden Place before the 1914 war.

Writing in the 1960s of her childhood memories, she gives a picture of a child's life cocooned with all the comforts of wealth, not far away from a street where half-starved

Walden Place.

children ran about bare-footed in rags. And her own devoted Nanny and an army of servants, both indoor and outdoor, made life easy for those whom they considered their superiors.

It is nevertheless a charming account of a vanished world, where a pony, wearing little leather boots over his hooves, pulled the lawn-mower in summer. When the mistress of the house went "calling" on certain afternoons during the week in a brougham driven by a coachman in buff livery and black top hat.

It describes in detail the "Cinderella Ball", held one Saturday evening in Walden Place (all the dancing had to end by midnight - it being Sunday the following morning). With the food - creamy trifles, jellies and cutlets with little paper frills - laid out on tables on the landing. And the gaslights burning brightly in all the rooms, whilst dancing couples twirled in the drawing room to the sound of music from the orchestra in the dining room.

She writes of Sundays, when she was allowed to have lunch with her adopted parents, and given Edinburgh rock to eat in the drawing room afterwards whilst mummy played the piano and daddy sang.

And of another thrilling event - the Garden Fête - held one warm sunny day, with the Town Band playing in their red and gold uniforms, conducted by the imposing figure of Mr. Pitstow, on the lawn in front of the house. With a "bicycle, gymkhana" and a children's Fancy-dress parade as special attractions. And - as dusk fell - paper Chinese lanterns strung across the pond, glowing gently in the near darkness.

But by Easter 1914 the hey-day of Walden Place came to an end. William Favill Tuke moved his family, servants and animals to Norcott Court near Berkhamstead, and the house was sold to the Red Cross for a Hospital during the troubled times which followed.

After the war it reverted to a private residence, and became the home of Mr. and Mrs. W.M. de Paula. But after the death of Mr. de Paula sometime in the 1970s, the house was again sold, this time to Uttlesford District Council for conversion into sheltered accommodation for the elderly.

Now the handsome drawing room - where graceful

couples once danced to the music of their time, watched by a wide-eyed little girl with snowdrops in her hair - is a residents' sitting room with a television set in one corner. The upstairs rooms, including the nurseries, and the study where Mr. and Mrs. Tuke would sit in the evenings, have all been transformed into self-contained flats.

More self-contained units have been built in part of the gardens where, Smith the gardener, and his underlings once worked, and a little girl sat in a summer house listening to her nurse's stories.

Little of that golden age, apart from the structure of the house itself, remains. Nevertheless Walden Place has a lightness and brightness seldom found in old buildings, and is still a very comfortable place to live. And the Town band still plays on the lawn in front of the house on summer afternoons - so the resident warden, Mrs. Miriam Hardwick told me.

Lancashire-born Mrs. Hardwick has been a warden for Uttlesford District Council since 1985, and she and her ex-Coldstream Guards husband - Joseph - have lived in Walden Place since January 1987.

CHAPTER EIGHT

Park Lane

First published in the Saffron Walden Weekly News
November 22 – December 6, 1990

Pedestrians and motorists alike take their lives into their hands when they brave the hazards of Park Lane. This narrowest of thoroughfares - which in fact, does not lead to any park - is one of the busiest in town. Little more than an alleyway between the Post Office and the Co-op Supermarket, it leads into ill-fated Swan Meadow and the Almshouses in Abbey Lane.

As part of the medieval core of Saffron Walden it has enjoyed various names throughout its long history. In 1400 it was Daniels Lane, by 1600 this had changed to Fullers Lane, presumably because of the fullers using the springs in Swan Meadow and Freshwell Street. Almost a hundred years later the name was changed again to Almshouse Lane which remained until about fifty years ago when, for whatever reason it became Park Lane.

Number 1 Park Lane is described in Department of Environment notes as "an early 19th century gault brick House, now painted". It was for many years the home of the writer, Mrs. Dorothea Wallis, now living in Thaxted.

Just recently, however, I discovered a hair-raising story in connection with this house. But just how true it is I really cannot say.

A certain baker, famed for his meat pies, ran his business at No.1 Park Lane, until it was discovered that he had committed several murders and he was finally hanged on Market Hill. Rumour had it that he used the bodies of his victims to make his meat pies!

Research has found no evidence to support this macabre story, which has a strong Sweeney Todd flavour. But certainly No.1 was a bakehouse and is listed in the rating lists for 1840 as such. The baker at that time was Charles Watson, who operated from 1840 until about 1856. And there is nothing to suggest that he was other than respectable as I am sure were his successors, Thomas Barnard and Obadiah Bush.

Obadiah Bush bought the business in 1860 and continued until 1891, when it was purchased by a Mr. David Miller, who later moved his business to London Road and died, a much respected member of the community, at the age of 75. (Down Your Street - Part Two - pages 154-155).

Number 1 continued to be a bakehouse until the turn of the century, when for a short time it was owned by Benjamin Cro, proprietor of Cro's Stores in the High Street.

So just who was the Demon Baker of Park Lane and when did he operate his nefarious trade?

No. 1 Park Lane – once a bakehouse.

188

However Park Lane has also pleasanter associations and is now irrevocably linked with the world of art thanks to the late Edward Bawden. This distinguished artist, who died a few months ago at the age of 86, spent the last 20 years of his life at No.2 Park Lane.

He was a former trustee of the Tate Gallery, and a senior Royal Academician. He was born in Braintree, and lived nearly all his life in Essex. For a number of years, he was the pivot of the Bardfield artistic community, but later, after the death of his wife, Charlotte, he moved to Saffron Walden.

An ex-pupil of the Friends' School during the first World War, he went on to study at the Cambridge School of Art and Technology then the Royal College of Art. His first public exhibition was held in London during the 1920s when he sold his paintings for six guineas each.

As an official war artist during the second World War he witnessed the evacuation of Dunkirk. Later, he was in a ship which got torpedoed, and after spending five days in an open boat, was picked up by the Vichy French and interned for three months in North Africa.

He was a prolific artist and produced literally hundreds of water colours, murals, prints and illustrations. Examples of his work are to be found in the permanent collection of North West Essex Artists at The Fry Art Gallery in Saffron Walden and various private and public Art Galleries throughout the country, including the Imperial War Museum.

———— • ————

Number 6 Park Lane is the home of Professor "Freddie" Marshall and his wife Olga. Although their house is modern, it is, in fact, built out of old tiles and bricks - some Tudor, some very soft clay, believed to have come from the Brickyard at Audley End.

When they bought the land 35 years ago it included the stables to No.7 High Street, former home of Miss Edith Tuke. The stables were actually an enormous Tythe Barn with a Georgian brick front and massive early 17th century timbers. It was big enough to accommodate six horses, three either

189

side with a large central area for carriages. But because the back of the barn was 18 feet lower than street level, permission to convert it into a dwelling was not granted.

There was nothing else for it but to pull the old barn down and incorporate as much of the materials as possible in a new house. Apart from the sheer hard work, the Marshalls were also very conscious that they were pulling down history. They had previously been told that the barn had belonged, at one time, to the Quaker, Anthony Pennystone who, during the persecution of the Quakers in Walden during the 17th century - "buried his wife like a dog in the garden."

Fortunately or unfortunately, the Marshalls did not uncover Mrs. Pennystone as they uprooted the 33 mature fruit trees which once comprised Miss Tuke's orchard.

After two years the house was finally completed, since when it has been the family home for the Marshalls and their four children.

Professor Marshall (who was actually christened, Norman Bertram) is a former Head of the Zoology and Comparative Physiology Department at Queen Mary College, University of London - now Professor Emeritus.

He was born in Little Shelford in 1915, and is a graduate of Downing College Cambridge. Before the war, from 1937 until 1941 he was Plankton Biologist in the Department of Oceanography at Hull University.

During the second World War he was in Army Operational Research, and later seconded to operation Tabarin in the Antarctic. By this time he was married to Olga, whom he had met in Yorkshire. (They had actually been introduced to each other by Dr. Jacob Bronowski.) Olga joined the W.R.N.S. in order to be near Freddie in London, but despite this, their marriage was only nine days old when he was sent off to the Antarctic.

They did not see each other for the next 20 months, and could only communicate with each other through a list of especially selected phrases 'none of which were appropriate to us.'

Once a month Olga would receive a telegram saying - the party known as N.B. Marshall when last reported was alive and well on - such and such a date. 'It was,' they say, 'real cloak and dagger stuff!'

After the war Freddie worked on Marine Fishes in the British Museum Natural History Department until 1972 when he took up his position at Queen Mary College.

During all this time he had been in charge of various expeditions, notably the Manihine Expedition to the Red Sea 1948-50 and the Te Vega Expedition 1966-67.

During his long career he has deservedly collected a number of awards, including the Polar Silver Medal and the Rosenthal Gold Medal for distinguished service to Marine Science, and perhaps not the least - a mountain which bears his name - Marshall Peak - in Antarctica.

As for Olga's career, she happily admits that, 'marriage has been my career. I think running a home and bringing up a family is extremely important, and I know if I had chosen a career I would never have married.'

So speaks a woman who types her husband's manuscripts, illustrates his books, acts as chauffeuse, accompanies him whenever she can, and has herself written and illustrated nine books on Natural History 'in between doing the ironing'. Add to this the creative ability to build an exact replica of No.6 Park Lane, reproducing all the furniture in every detail, including her husband's library, complete with books, which includes, probably the last painting ever by Edward Bawden - a miniature of his cats!

Anyone visiting No.8 Park Lane - the home of Mr. and Mrs. James Case - is sure to be warmly greeted by their spaniel Max.

Nine years-old Max is just one in a long series of pets owned by the Case's during their fifty years of marriage. Dogs, monkeys, rats and even snakes have all earned a place in their affections.

James and Betty Case have lived at No.8 Park Lane since 1977. However their association with the town goes much further back than that, back to the year before the second World War when Betty's father - F.B. Malim, retired Master of Wellington College - brought his family to live at Myddylton House.

Betty and her brothers and sisters - all eight of them -

were the first young people to move into the town for many years and were showered with invitations.

Betty, a keen sportswoman, played Lacrosse for England, and Squash for the County, but also enjoyed a good game of tennis. Nearly every Saturday morning she could be found playing tennis on the hard court owned by shoe-shop proprietor, Mr. Wally de Barr at No.3 Park Lane. (Down Your Street - Part One - pages 28-29).

It was at a tennis party, given by their next-door neighbours, the de Paula's, that she met her husband. At that time James, a young Army Captain stationed at Debden, was also very keen on sport. They married in 1940 and their eldest son Oliver, was born at Myddylton House in 1942. But very shortly afterwards the young couple moved to Bishop's Stortford, where they continued to live until 1961 when they returned to Myddylton House to look after Betty's recently widowed father.

James retired from the Stock Exchange in 1977, by which time both their sons were grown up, and they were finding Myddylton House far too big for their requirements. It was then that they saw great possibilities in the gardener's cottage belonging to Walden Place.

The gardener's cottage had been built in 1925, to house a horse as well as a gardener and possessed only the minimum conveniences. The bathroom, served as a kitchen with an old door covering the bath for a kitchen table. But it did have four good rooms, two of them very nicely-sized, and the Case's felt that they could do a lot with it.

It took nine months to enlarge and convert before they could move in just before Christmas 1977. The next year they turned their attention to the garden, which, even on a day dripping with November gloom, looks absolutely charming.

Although the Case's are not local people in the strictest sense of the word, they have nevertheless, integrated themselves into the life of the community.

Since 1978, James has been Treasurer of the Home Farm Trust at Orford House. He is also a member of the Conservative Club, and an extremely long-standing member of the Golf Club. His first game of golf was played there in

1938 when camping at Audley End with the Territorials. (His service with the Territorial Army lasted 12 years and earned him the Territorial Decoration).

Betty was a local Magistrate for over 22 years, something she says she enjoyed very much. She has also been a former Chairman of the local branch of the Arthritis and Rheumatism Council, and is now their President, and also serves on the Committee of St. Marks College at Audley End.

Living where they do, the subject of the proposed Swan Meadow Car Park inevitably surfaces. James summed up their feelings by saying 'it will be murder for us! We will have the lights on nearly all night long. And it will be a waste of money, it will be nothing but a white elephant.'

Judging from the number of stickers I saw in the windows of their neighbours, I felt that the Case's were not alone in their feelings, and I couldn't help wondering how many Councillors would welcome a Car Park next door to their home?

Benten & Co

Certified Accountants
Registered Auditors

*Offering friendly, helpful advice on all taxation
and accountancy matters.*

**Abbey House, 51 High Street, Saffron Walden.
Telephone : (01799) 523053**

CHAPTER NINE

Abbey Lane

First published in the Saffron Walden Weekly News
January 3 – February 28, 1991

Stand in Abbey Lane and you stand on the very foundations of the history of Saffron Walden.

It has been written:- "that there is no lack of archaeological evidence showing the presence of man in this area (Abbey Lane and Elm Grove) from at least neolithic times." It is also believed that a small Roman fort was sited to the south of Abbey Lane, close to the cemetery excavated by George Stacey Gibson in 1876, (the vicinity of the Gibson housing estate). A later excavation in 1975, though disappointing, provided enough evidence to encourage future investigation.

As the Abbey Lane area together with Audley End and Little Walden comprised three important communities along the main trade routes above the River Cam, it does seem reasonable to assume that probably Abbey Lane is the oldest thoroughfare in the town.

In 1136 a Priory was founded in this area, later to become a Benedictine Abbey, from which the name Abbey Lane is derived. The Abbey was superseded in 1616 by the mansion we know as Audley End House, built by Thomas, 1st Earl of Suffolk.

Perhaps the most important feature of present day Abbey Lane is the large, early 19th century building known as King Edward VI's Almshouses. These Almshouses were built in 1834 to replace earlier ones.

The very first Almshouse:- "in sustenation of 13 poor men and women" - was built in 1400 on the orchard of Roger de

The "new" Almshouses, built in 1834.

Walden, Archbishop of Canterbury, in what is now Park
Lane. Now, the whole almshouse complex joining Park Lane
with Abbey Lane represents the replacement and extension
of the original one, updated and modernised and in recent
years, augmented by purpose-built flats and bungalows.

Some links with the past are still retained however, and in
the Almshouse Trustees' Room there can be found an
ancient brass plate to commemorate Thomas Byrd:- "out of
whose goods this fire-hearth was erected".

The Byrd family, one of the most notable families since the
reign of Richard II in Walden and Littlebury, reached their
zenith in Tudor times. They are believed to have been
dispossessed of their lands during Cromwell's time, and
nothing now remains to remind us of them except a
memorial in the church and - Byrd's Farm.

Unfortunately, the most treasured link with a former
Almshouse benefactor was sold for £2,900 at Christie's on
July 31, 1929. Repairs to the roof of the Almshouses were
urgently needed, and despite both local and national
protests the Trustees decided to sell the Pepys Mazer Bowl.

The Mazer Bowl, a small maplewood bowl, less than 8 inches in diameter with a plain silver-gilt rim and a circular, engraved silver plate at the base, was presented to the Almshouses probably in the 15th century by Margaret Bregchman.

The exact purpose of the Mazer is not clear, and it is generally assumed that it was intended for religious purposes which, with passing years, became merely ceremonial.

Originally the inmates were given a pail of beer once a year and each drank his share from the Mazer. Later, only the Trustees drank from it, each paying the Town Crier a shilling as he passed it around. In more recent times, the Mazer was kept in the bank because by this time it leaked, and when it was handed around it was filled with ten shilling notes.

It was Samuel Pepys who gave the Mazer its historical significance when he visited the Almshouse on February 27, 1660, during a brief stay in the town. He records in his diary for that date that:- "they brought me a draught in a brown bowl, tipt with silver, which I drank of, and at the bottom was a picture of the Virgin and the Child in her arms, done in silver."

It does seem however, that for a large part of its life the Mazer bowl was more or less forgotten until the decision to sell it. It was bought by a silver dealer who re-sold it again to an American banker for £6,000. Forty years later, to the astonishment of everyone concerned, the Mazer reappeared in a catalogue of a sale of old silver at Christie's on June 23, 1971. This time it fetched £22,000.

It did return to Walden for a very short spell in 1986 as part of the Charter 750 celebrations. But the prospect of it ever returning to the town on a more permanent basis is now beyond the realms of feasibility. Those interested however, may see a replica of the bowl in the Museum.

The Almshouses are no longer an institution of charity, they have been divided into comfortable, modern, self-contained homes, providing sheltered accommodation for elderly people born in the town. All residents lead completely independent lives, but have the security of knowing that help is within call should it be needed.

"Master of the Almshouse and his Part-Brother" sounds a bit archaic but rather more picturesque than "Chairman and Vice-Chairman of the Gibson Charity". The titles - which apply respectively to Mr. Brian Newman and Mr. Denis Weaver - do however, amount to one and the same thing.

"The Master and his Part-Brother" are titles which most probably date back to the very first Almshouse built in 1400. And archaic though this mode of address might be, it is one which Brian Newman feels must be perpetuated even if only used occasionally for historical purposes.

Brian Newman has been Master of the Almshouse for the past 20 years. As Managing Director of James Jewellers, of King Street, he is carrying on a long-established tradition which goes back to the days when all the Almshouse Trustees were local tradespeople.

The Matron, deputy Matron and Clerk, are all responsible to the Master, and as well as chairing the Trustee Meetings, he is also concerned with the secular welfare of the residents. Every Sunday morning, after attending the 8 o'clock Service at St. Mary's, Brian Newman can be seen walking in the grounds of the Almshouses, meeting and talking to as many residents as he possibly can.

Mr. Newman assured me that all the residents live most harmoniously together and frequently help each other out. 'Sometimes this involves doing a bit of shopping or perhaps just having a cup of tea and a chat together. This is something we actively encourage and has been very successful. There really is a very lovely atmosphere.'

The residents' physical welfare is the concern of the Almshouse Matron - 27 year-old Mrs. Tracey Scott. There are 46 residents in her care, aged between 60 and 95, and by means of a sophisticated alarm system she is on call all day long - even when asleep!

Major John Streatfeild, Clerk to the Almshouse Trustees, describes himself 'as the other half of the Matron.' It is his responsibility to ensure the smooth-running of the Almshouses which includes the finances. In this respect he says he is helped by Mr. Denis Weaver, 'who is a great financial expert.'

Major Streatfeild has been the Clerk to the Almshouse Trustees since 1st April 1988, when the previous Clerk - Miss Martin - expressed a wish to retire. As he had previously been involved with the Almshouses when serving as a Borough Councillor 18 years ago, he was asked if he would like to take her place.

He explained that the Almshouses - whose correct title is "King Edward VI and the Rev. Joseph Prime Almshouse Charity" - are a privately run organisation. And although not strictly a Charity in the original sense, it is part of the Gibson Charity which is also administered by Major Streatfeild.

——— • ———

'I used to sing in the choir at Abbey Lane' or 'I belong to Abbey Lane, I've belonged there ever since I was a child' are words frequently uttered by members of the older generation in Saffron Walden when reminiscing. They never add the word "church"; they know it isn't necessary, everyone knows what they mean.

Space does not permit a detailed history of this nonconformist church, but those interested will find the Town Library a valuable source of information.

Abbey Lane Congregational Church.

However it is interesting to note that the present building with its austere elegance and Ionic four-column portico was built in 1811 to replace an early late 17th century chapel. The latter, in turn, replaced a barn which stood on this site where early Dissenters in the town first met to worship.

A splendid feature of the church's interior is the mahogany pulpit with its sweeping staircase. This is believed to be older than the present church, and has been described as an example of "fine 18th century craftsmanship."

But the United Reformed Church in Abbey Lane is not just a building, it has an extremely active congregation, despite the fact that for the past two years the Church has had to rely upon lay-preachers, visiting ministers and Dr. James Anderson of Cambridge to take their Sunday morning Services.

'At the moment the Church is run by a very efficient body of Elders,' said a spokesperson, 'plus a marvellous Fabric Committee who do so many of the repairs, and other willing helpers.'

Some of these helpers include an indefatigable group of ladies who make all sorts of delicious refreshments for various functions in the town. By this means they help to raise funds for their Church, and no occasion is too big for them to buckle to and get out their mixing bowls.

Standing to one side and a little behind the Church, is the Church Hall. This is a venue for all sorts of activities connected with the town, not the least of these being the Abbey Lane Play School.

The school which is open five days a week from 9.30 until 12 noon, is registered to take 32 children, and is entirely self-supporting financed from proceeds of a Jumble Sale held once a year and the fees charged per session.

Although Abbey Lane is dominated by two architectural focal points - the Almshouses and the United Reformed Church - it also possesses other interesting features worthy of note.

Opposite the Almshouses and backing on to the gardens of the houses of Gibson Close, there is a fine example of The Battle Ditches. These Ditches, attributed to Humphrey de

Bohun, 2nd Earl of Hereford, 7th Earl of Essex, are assumed to have been constructed in the 13th century. The Abbey Lane Saxon settlement, forerunner of present-day Walden, having passed into the hands of the Normans soon after the Conquest.

Geoffrey de Mandeville, close friend of the Conqueror, is believed to have been the first Norman to take up residence here. Then perhaps realizing the strategic importance of nearby Bury Hill, encouraged development towards that site.

Humphrey de Bohun, who inherited the title in 1236, might have thought that the construction of the Ditches would help to limit the spread of the community in the Abbey Lane area, forcing further development towards the region of Bury Hill. Humphrey also granted certain rights in property to encourage settlement in the new town, laying-out a grid pattern of plots which he hoped would interest newcomers.

Probably, also around this time, the earliest church - now believed to have stood on the Abbey Lane site - was moved to Bury Hill. This would have provided further incentive for the population to move north-east.

Gibson Close and its neighbours is also the site of the Saxon Cemetery excavated by George Stacey Gibson in 1876. Those interested will find two of the skeletons (both "gentlemen") from this Cemetery in the Saffron Walden Museum, in specially constructed illuminated cases sunk into the floor of the new Archaeological Section of the Museum.

On the eastern side of the United Reformed Church is another group of Almshouses. These are the Gibson Free Dwellings. These houses were especially built by the Gibson family for their former employees.

Continuing on our way we arrive at all that remains of the clubhouse of the Town Bowling Club. The Saffron Walden Town Bowling Club moved here in 1949 from their old Green behind the Rose & Crown in the Market Place. It is believed that the Club was first inaugurated there in 1896. But now members believe that the time has come for a new clubhouse, and the great thing is, the whole operation is

The old clubhouse of the Town Bowling Club.

being done by the members of the Bowling Club themselves! After the last game of bowls was played on the last Sunday in September last year, those members who were able - reported for work the very next morning and started to demolish the old wooden clubhouse. And by the time the bowling season starts again in April 1991, Saffron Walden Town Bowling Club will have a brand new clubhouse!

It seems there is a lot of talent - apart from bowling - in the club - brick-layers, carpenters, electricians, and other than perhaps a few specialist jobs, no outside contracters will be used. Those who are not skilled artizans, will happily work as labourers. Team spirit in every sense of the word!

Now, walking right to the end of Abbey Lane we come to the entrance to the Park of Audley End Mansion, and here we find Walden Lodge.

Built like a tiny Gothic castle in buff gault brick, with a picturesque turret, Walden Lodge is one of the numerous gate houses belonging to the Audley End estate. Low down on one of the walls of the house the date 1814 can be seen.

This is believed to be the date of the house which is rather surprising as the architectural Gothic revival, influenced by Pugin, was actually much later on in the 19th century.

Retracing our steps, we pass more sheltered accommodation for the elderly - Parkside and Hanover Housing - and approach the High Street to find that the lane gets less residential and more commercial. Perhaps this is not surprising because, between 1856 and 1869 one of the numerous town maltings stood on the site now occupied by two private car parks.

The malting, owned by Mr. R.W. Spicer and operated by Robert Fitch, was acquired by the Gibsons in 1869 and sometime later closed down. Rating lists for 1875 describe it as being empty, and in 1877 "workshops and yard".

Rating lists also reveal that it was here, in a cottage (No.2 or 3 Abbey Lane) that the very first Infants' School was set up. The cottage was also a Gibson property and the school appears to have been run by a Mrs. Rumsey from 1839 until 1849. After that time the school in Museum Street - built in 1817 and forerunner of the National School in Castle Street - became officially designated as an Infants' School, and the one in Abbey Lane appears in the rating lists as empty.

The bustle of the High Street begins to make its presence felt as we come to the parade of modern shops in Abbey Lane.

Walden Lodge.

203

CHAPTER TEN

George Street

First published in the Saffron Walden Weekly News
January 17 – March 7, 1991

George Street - less picturesque than its close neighbours, thanks to unsympathetic development - is a street of small shops and businesses still retaining something of the flavour of old Walden in that most of the businesses are individually owned.

The origins of the name George Street appear to be lost in obscurity. In the early 17th century it was Clothiers Lane, later, on the town map of 1758 it is shown as a continuation of Hill Street, and early rating lists show it as George Lane. Perhaps it became George Lane when the George Public House came into being in 1786.

The George stood on the corner of Gold Street and George Street - now the site of an Indian Restaurant - with its stables spreading westwards along the street almost meeting up with the stables from the Greyhound on the corner of High Street and George Street. Separating each set of stables was - conveniently placed - a smithy!

Fortunately for us, the Greyhound - an attractive 17th century building - still stands, although it has long ceased to function as an inn and now houses the Weekly News Office and an Opticians.

Unhappily, the stables belonging to the Greyhound like those of the George, were demolished in the early sixties along with the smithy to make way for a parade of shops. From this we may gather that George Street at the beginning of the century looked rather different from the George Street we know today.

George Street – 1980.

A hundred years ago Willetts butcher's shop (now Walden Models) would have stood on the corner opposite the Greyhound. Next door at Nos. 2 and 3 would have been Mr. Charles Hagger's antique shop. (Now B.J.T. telephones and an estate agents).

Charles Hagger first establisbed his antique business at Nos. 41-43 Castle Street, later moving to Nos. 2 and 3 George Street in 1886 and an adjacent property - Wedds coachbuilders' showroom in January 1892.

(Wedds coachbuilders was the site of the old candle factory mentioned on the 1877 map of Saffron Walden.)

He hadn't been in George Street long before he extended his premises to Nos. 4, 5, and 6 - thus owning the whole of the northern side of George Street from beyond the butcher's shop on the corner right down as far as a carriage-way arch.

Entrance to Nos. 2 and 3 - where Charles and his family lived, and which also served as an office - was through a tiny yard, filled with potted plants. And many people must still remember the railings surmounting the low wall and

206

the wrought-iron gate which opened out on to George Street.

Some of Charles Hagger's stock came from Sotheby's and Christie's in London, and many of his customers were members of the aristocracy. A carriage and pair outside Charles Hagger's showroom was a familiar sight in George Street in the early decades of this century! Nor were his customers purely local people. Records show that purchases were sent all over the country as well as abroad.

A lot of his success was due to the fact that he employed his nephew, Charles Wright, who was an expert carpenter and restorer.

Charles Hagger and his wife, Emily, had six children, Edward, James, Agnes, Ingram, Christopher and Violet. But only Agnes remained in Saffron Walden to support her parents. Edward and Christopher emigrated to Australia, James joined the Royal Navy and later worked for the Foreign Section of the G.P.O., Ingram became a Sales Rep in the Perfumery Trade and Violet married a chartered surveyor and went to live in Southampton.

Mr. Charles Hagger outside his shop in George Street, about 1920.

Charles enjoyed a deep and lasting friendship with two other wellknown gentlemen in the town, Ernest Hart - the Stationer in King Street - and Arthur Midgley of Larchmount, London Road. And even to this day, his grandson, Mr. Jack Hagger, has in his possession two of Ernest Hart's personal diaries. In one of them, an entry for 20th August 1886 states "bought table at Hagger's for £2."

Another treasured possession of Jack Hagger's is "The Hagger Family Loving Cup." This is a large and splendid double handled mug, made by Arthur Midgley in 1914 at his kiln in Bovey-Tracey in Devon. It is a fine example of white ceramic decorated in blue and white with the date of Charles and Emily's marriage and the birth dates of their six children.

Charles Hagger obviously enjoyed his patriarchal role, for in 1925 he achieved his ambition which was to gather together all his seven grandchildren. He paid all their expenses, which included fares for young Charles junior and Agnes junior (Girlie) in Australia, and brought them all to Saffron Walden for a holiday. Four years later he died.

After his death it was revealed, that he had been a great local benefactor, and had contributed generously to many worthy causes.

Emily and her daughter Agnes, carried on the business until 1940, when Emily decided to retire at the age of 82. They moved to 57 High Street, where Emily died in 1949 aged 91. Agnes herself lived until 1967, dying at the age of 85.

The foregoing information was given to me by Charles Hagger's grandson Mr. Jack Hagger of Victoria Avenue.

Jack himself was born in London but spent most of his school holidays in Saffron Walden at his grandparents house in George Street. He says his earliest memories of George Street are of playing "bat and ball" in the road outside his grandfather's shop, and Gus Britton's butcher's shop on the corner (previously Willets.)

It was always his ambition to live in Walden. This was realised when, after his mother's death in 1939, his father remarried and moved to the town. Jack was called up and served in the army during the second World War, but came back to Walden after he was demobbed. By this time he had married his one and only sweetheart - Dorothy, a London girl - and as a married man he settled down to a career in the Gas Industry, eventually becoming Fens Area Personnel Manager. He and Dorothy moved to Victoria Avenue in 1947, where he has remained ever since. Sadly, Dorothy died eight years ago.

Now Jack enjoys his retirement alone, by 'filling my head with snippets of useless information' (he has a phenomenal memory for numbers) doing crossword puzzles and being Vice-President of the Cambridge Gas Employees Sports Club.

———— • ————

At a time when Saffron Walden appears to be losing all its long-established family businesses, it is encouraging to find a new one flourishing. Grayson and Start, Family Butchers, at No.9 George Street are a family business in the true sense, run by local people.

Mr. Terry Start, a member of the wellknown Start family, was born in East Street in a tiny row of cottages opposite the Waggon and Horses. (The cottages were demolished in the 1950s and replaced by flower beds.) Like so many local businessmen, he started his education at Museum Street School, progressed to St. Mary's in Castle Street and completed his education at The County High. After leaving school at the age of 15 he went to work for Goddards the butchers in Church Street.

When Goddards closed in September 1988, he and Mrs. Isobel Grayson, decided to open up their own business. Mrs. Grayson is the wife of Terry's nephew, Robin Grayson - thus the family connection. Robin himself, is engaged in another branch of the family business - building - which doesn't mean he isn't called upon to help out when things get hectic at Grayson and Start!

It takes a lot of courage to open a business these days but since they opened just over two years ago, Grayson and Start have become a household word in the town. Much of their success can be attributed to the fact that most of the

Isobel Grayson (on bike), Terry Start (extreme left) and staff.

staff have been in the butchery trade all their working lives. In fact, all but one member of their seven fulltime staff are 'ex-Goddard boys' says Mrs. Grayson.

To augment experience gained from the past, Isobel and Terry have encouraged their assistants to attend Courses at Smithfield College in London. Also, to keep pace with modern trends, they have a full range of free-range meat, purchased from The Real Meat Company, one of the top names in free-range meat production. This is something, Isobel says, they are happy to offer their customers 'although,' she adds, 'we are very lucky because we do know where all our meat comes from!'

All the meat sold is cut by hand, as are all the sausages tied by hand. And just as Goddards' sausages were famed all over the Saffron Walden area, so now are Grayson and Starts'. Last year, Terry came first in the East of England Sausage Making Competition, and was recently one of the top 24 sausage-makers from all over the country taking part in a competition held at the Butchers' Hall in London.

'We did not win,' says Isobel, 'but it was great fun and we did have lunch with Barbara Windsor who was the Celebrity Judge.'

Loafers Bakery is one of three shop units at No.15 George Street which were once part of Mr. Charles Hagger's antique showrooms, later Choppens D.I.Y. and hardware shop for about 40 years. (Down Your Street - Part Two - pages 48-51).

Although not strictly a family business, Loafers is, nevertheless, a true local business, run by local people whose roots are firmly planted in the past. Mr. Bill Banks and his partners, Mr. John Freeman and Mr. Graham Ball, have all, at sometime in their lives, worked for Millers the Bakers. (Down Your Street - Part Two - pages 154-155).

When Millers sold out to Dorringtons about four years ago, Bill and his partners decided to pool their expertise and open up their own bakery. After three years of extremely hard work, they now have the satisfaction of knowing that their venture has been an unqualified success. Now they would dearly love to expand but unfortunately, like a lot of small businesses, they find the rents in the town so exorbitant that this is impossible.

Fifty-one year-old Bill Banks was born in Stocks Yard at the top of the High Street. He was one of the first batch of intakes at the County Technical School (now The County High), and when he left school at the age of 15 he went straight to Millers' Bakery in London Road. At the same time he attended Cambridge College of Arts and Technology on a day-release basis.

Altogether he spent five years at Cambridge C.A.T. learning to be a Master Baker, a Course which his two partners also undertook. Eventually both his partners spread their wings by working for other bakers in the town, but Bill remained at Millers.

Bakers work long, unsociable hours. Bill and his partners start work at three o'clock in the morning and continue until ten or ten-thirty. Which means that they spend most afternoons sleeping. On Fridays, work begins at seven-thirty in the evening and goes on until five o'clock Saturday morning.

Unsociable hours don't seem to worry Bill however, although he admits that Carol, his wife, 'does get fed up at times!'

All the bread at Loafers is baked on the premises, and all

Bill Banks (centre) and partners.

the loaves are moulded by hand. 'We have only one machine used for the bread and that is the actual mixer. We really are old-fashioned bakers in the true sense of the word,' says Bill.

With 36 years in the Trade, Bill has seen a lot of changes. He remembers the time when he would go up to Millers' Bakery in London Road on Christmas Day to cook turkeys for some of their customers. 'Now, of course we couldn't do that, the ovens we use are not tall enough.'

He has also seen big changes in people's eating habits. 'Over the last 20 years sales of bread have been going down. People no longer have bread, butter and cake for tea, they usually have a cooked meal instead. And working men no longer take sandwiches for their lunch.

Now we make more small loaves than large, and sell more french sticks than small loaves. And we make far more rolls than we did in the old days. We also find we sell a lot of wholemeal bread and Oast House loaves - a type of granary bread.'

One of the six fulltime staff employed by Loafers is Mrs. Linda Porter, an ex-Millers' Bakery employee - 'right from leaving school' - who joined Loafers as soon as it opened.

Leaving Loafers with its delicious smell of baking bread we come to the carriage-way which leads to the Glasswells' furniture store in King Street.

Glasswells, was founded in Bury St. Edmunds in 1946, and a branch opened in Saffron Walden in 1951. Recently they have enlarged their premises to include a separate carpet and curtain department in a building at the entrance to the carriage-way.

Many older readers will remember this yard in the days of Robson & Sons - the old established business, founded in 1760 by Thomas Day and his wife, Susanna, as a grocers, drapers and general stores. Gradually with the passing years and various marriages, the name changed but the business remained virtually in the hands of the same family. (Down Your Street - Part One - page 85).

By 1886 - Robson & Sons - a household name in Walden, flourished on both sides of King Street, with a warehouse in Station Road, and an army of horses, carts and delivery vans. Some of the horses were stabled in the yard opening on to George Street. And what is now the carpet and curtain department of Glasswells was a small cottage belonging to Robsons, the home of Mr. and Mrs. Cowells.

Just a little further along George Street there used to be a little sweet shop run at one time by a Mrs. Whitehead. After the first World War this little shop was taken over by Mr. Frank Ketteridge who established a shoe shop with a shoe-repairing workshop next door. The sweet shop is now Bonkers, a trendy clothing shop for ladies, but the shoe-repairing business still flourishes, although it has changed hands at least twice since those early days.

Essex Shoe Repairs, managed by 23 year-old Karl Hunnings, has been operating from 17a George Street for three years now. All that time Karl has been in charge, and since then the volume of business has increased by a hundred percent.

Karl has been in the shoe repairing business ever since he left school in Peterborough. He now lives in Saffron

213

Walden, a decision he took to be near his fiancé and also because he felt he wanted 'to try a new way of life!'

Certainly he must find living and working in Walden very different from Peterborough where, he says, 'people believe in doing what they want to do.' Whereas, according to Karl, Saffron Walden is a very sleepy little town and the people who live in it are very 'traditional.'

This very refreshingly honest comment from someone who has elected to live in the town was augmented by the opinion of 16 year-old Simon Curtis. Simon, who lives in Bishop's Stortford, is training to mend shoes under Karl's expert eye. He openly admits that he hasn't really got used to Saffron Walden yet and really prefers Bishop's Stortford because, 'there's more to do in Stortford!'

Besides mending shoes, Karl assured me that they 'will have a go at mending anything, be it a handbag or purse, belt or whatever.' He also added that people need not be afraid of bringing in something which has seen better days, 'I can assure you that no matter how old or shabby it is - we've always seen worse!'

——— • ———

Undoubtedly the presence of the smithy, on the southern side of George Street, made a big commercial impact on the street during its lifetime. For the greater part of this century it was run by Mr. Frederick Bell and his son Hubert.

Frederick Bell, a Lancashire man, came to Saffron Walden in 1922. A highly skilled farrier and blacksmith, he took over the George Street smithy which had been established during the 17th century. It was a very large smithy - the shop itself reached halfway up Gold Street - and at one time contained six forges.

Only four forges remained when Frederick took over, and gradually over the years these were pulled down until only the original 17th century one was left.

In those days, the George Inn was a house one room wide, with a passage and an entrance at the back. The pillars and windows of the Indian Restaurant which replaced it did not exist, instead there was a plain brick wall.

Hubert Bell outside his forge in George Street 1920s/30s.

Frederick, his wife Maud and their son Hubert, lived in the Smith's house, an eight-roomed cottage, now the Oxfam shop.

Hubert Bell - now in his 80s - recalls what George Street was like in those days. He remembers the wooden framed cottages which stood on the corner of Gold Street, opposite the George. These were pulled down to make way for the Co-op, later Budgens, and now a development of small shop units.

The three stables belonging to the Greyhound (Weekly News Office) actually joined the blacksmith's shop, and The Greyhound had a cobbled yard with a horse trough standing in it. On market days the yard would be filled with ponies and traps, as well as lining the whole of George Street on one side right up to the market.

But the days of the pony and trap were numbered and with the coming of the second World War transport was becoming increasingly mechanised. Further, skilled metal-workers were needed for the War Effort and Hubert and his father found themselves working for the Government.

Frederick retired in 1944 and Hubert took over the business. But after the war, apart from a few farm horses, there was very little call for a skilled blacksmith. So Hubert decided to turn his hand to something different. The old forge was equipped with modern machinery, and it took on a fresh lease of life by manufacturing all kinds of metalwork.

Not only did Hubert provide the metalwork for practically the whole of Walden - lamp-posts, railings, steel work for the Parish Church roof and lamps for the Town Hall - but he also sent his wares all over the country.

Now Hubert is also retired, and his son, Keith, continues the business - Bell Precision Engineering - now based in Haverhill.

Hubert Bell has a keen historical interest in George Street, and tells the story of a one-time rival - the Fairycroft Forge. It seems that a hundred years ago, one, George Aldridge, worked in the George Street smithy for a man by the name of Chambers. One day Chambers lost his temper with Aldridge and hit him on the head with a rasp. Infuriated, Aldridge left Chambers and set up in opposition in

Fairycroft Road. (The Fairycroft Forge still stands but is now used by the Saffron Walden Operatic Society for storage purposes.)

Hubert was a member of the Saffron Walden Volunteer Fire Brigade for many years, during which time his heart was set on fire by a certain young lady called Gladys Barker.

Over fifty years ago, the Fire Brigade was called out to fight a factory fire at Littlebury, the village where Gladys lived. Gladys' mother made tea for the firemen and at the same time helped to brew-up a romance between her daughter and a certain young fireman!

Since the blacksmith's forge and the stables were demolished in the early sixties to make way for the parade of shops, many of them have changed hands time and time again. Not so -The Flower Shop!

Mr. Henry Welch, and his wife - aptly named - Heather, have been running The Flower Shop at No.6 George Street for 26 years. They claim - rightly - that they are now the only original business in the street.

When they first came, Brackens, the newsagents, was a shop selling animal feeding stuffs, and then later, Smiths Drycleaners. Pop In - the fashion shop was a little mini-market, then a shoe-shop, and the Oxfam shop was Fells the Chemists.

Henry and Heather, who live in Bishop's Stortford, were looking for a business in another town when No.6, previously called Pamela's, came on the market. They had been in agriculture but Henry had a leaning towards floristry.

Both he and Heather took courses on floristry to advance their skills when they opened-up their flower shop. And Henry can still remember vividly the first wreath he ever made - for a funeral in Thaxted.

Times have changed since those early days, and he no longer finds it necessary to get to Covent Garden Market by 3.30 in the morning - 4.00 am at the very latest - with the long drive back to Saffron Walden followed by a full day's work! Now, most of the flowers come from Holland and arrive at the door by van.

Customers' buying habits have changed also. Friday used

Henry and Heather Welch outside their flower shop.

to be the busiest day at The Flower Shop, now Monday is the busiest. This Henry puts down to the increasing number of people who spend the weekend staying with friends, and like to thank their hostesses with a bunch of flowers or a pot plant. Pot plants, apparently are becoming more and more popular. A habit he thinks we have picked up from the Continent.

Weddings and funerals, form a large part of the business at The Flower Shop, and all the time Henry was talking to me, his busy fingers were skilfully creating a wreath - almost without looking.

Here again, things have changed with the years. 'More oasis sprays are bought nowadays,' he says. 'Although we do get requests for unusual wreaths at times,' he shows me a block of oasis cut to form the letters "DAD". 'Sometimes we are asked for a wreath made to look like a dart board, or a rugby ball, and of course an anchor for an old sea salt, and sometimes sadly, one in the shape of a Teddy Bear.

Weddings, of course, are more joyous occasions and we usually do flowers for about 35 weddings a year.'

It was surprising to learn that not many young ladies fancy taking up floristry as a career these days. Why? 'Possibly because a flower shop is a very cold place to work in!'

Nevertheless, Ruth Gilder, who comes from Debden, has worked in The Flower Shop ever since she left school ten years ago, and has never regretted it. She loves her work, but admits that it took her about a year to learn the trade because - 'you have to go through all the seasons, to gain experience with all the different flowers.'

Next door to The Flower Shop we find The Voluntary Social Aid Shop. Voluntary Social Aid is a national charity with headquarters in Peterborough, registered in 1960.

The Charity now has shops selling good quality secondhand clothing, bric-a-brac, books and jewellery, all over the country. All the proceeds go towards helping people whose Social Security does not meet all their needs. Sometimes it is a matter of providing furniture and basic household goods, and at others perhaps, help financially.

Mrs. Ellen Clayden who runs the shop with the help of

219

other volunteers, told me that although they raise between £9,000 and £10,000 a year, the running costs of the shop are extremely high. 'There isn't much left after you have deducted rent and the business rate!'

Hair By Us is a bright, modern hairdressing salon above the parade. It is owned and run by two ladies who are very much local girls - Valerie Penning and Sue Barker. Valerie was born in nearby Ashdon and Sue in Wendens Ambo, both are ex-pupils of The County High School.

Although they knew each other at school, their friendship really started when they were serving their hairdressing apprenticeship at Maison Louise in Emson Close (later it became "Margarets"). They discovered they had a lot in common which, they felt, was an ideal basis for setting up in business together.

So in 1973 - by which time both girls were married - they opened their first hairdressing salon in a room in Valerie's bungalow in Radwinter. Right from the start the partnership was an outstanding success and within the short space of one year, they had moved into their present premises in George Street. Now they employ 20 staff and are proud to still have clients from their early days at Maison Louise.

Another important enterprise in George Street is, of course, the Oxfam Shop.

The local secretary of Oxfam - Maureen Evans - told me that the Saffron Walden branch of Oxfam was soon to celebrate its 20th anniversary. And that in the near future a second shop in King Street will be opened. With the result that the George Street branch will be run mainly as a secondhand book shop. So Oxfam will be looking for a lot more volunteers to help out.

At the moment Oxfam has about 60 volunteers who help both in the shop and behind the scenes. One of these is Flossie Gedney, who, now well into her eighties, spends every afternoon 'doing battle with the clothing in our very tiny sorting area', something Flossie has done ever since the shop first opened in town.

Maureen, Press Officer at Saffron Walden Museum, has been involved with Oxfam since 1964, and with the local

Flossie Gedney sorting clothes in the Oxfam shop.

group ever since she came to live in Saffron Walden 18 years ago. She told me that the Saffron Walden shop raises almost £100,000 a year and that over 90p in every pound raised goes to Oxford for relief and development work - mainly in Third World Countries, but also in this country as well. (Since the shop opened it has actually raised over three quarters of a million pounds).

Next door to Oxfam is all that is left of the old George Inn - the Nemonthron Indian Restaurant.

221